SPIRITUAL ABUSE
RECOVERY
WORKBOOK

SPIRITUAL ABUSE RECOVERY WORKBOOK

Engaging Faith in Healing

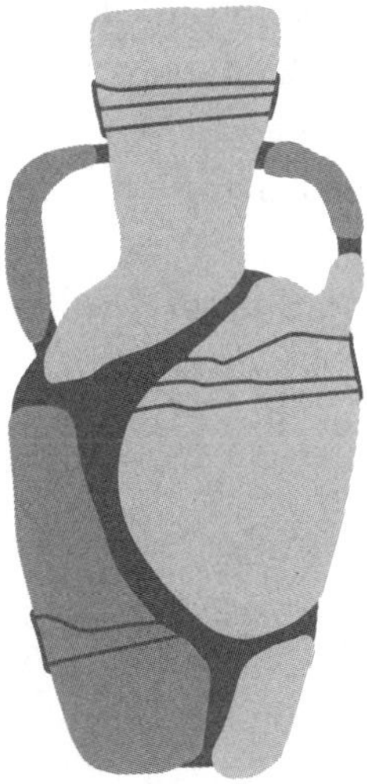

KAREN ROUDKOVSKI

B&H ACADEMIC®
BRENTWOOD, TENNESSEE

Spiritual Abuse Recovery Workbook

Published by B&H Academic®
Brentwood, Tennessee

ISBN: 978-1-4300-9156-1

Dewey Decimal Classification: 253.5
Subject Heading: CHRISTIANITY--PSYCHOLOGY
\ SPIRITUALITY \ SPIRITUAL LIFE

Cover design by Emily Keafer Lambright. Cover images by Larisa Rusina/iStock and LiuSol/iStock.

Printed in the United States of America

30 29 28 27 26 25 VP 1 2 3 4 5 6 7 8 9 10

CONTENTS

This workbook does not replace professional therapy, nor does the use of this workbook constitute a therapeutic relationship with the author, Karen Roudkovski.

AN INTRODUCTION

When I began writing *Understanding Spiritual Abuse*, I quickly realized that I wanted the book to have a companion workbook for spiritual-abuse survivors. Thankfully, my publisher agreed. If you are a Christian who has experienced spiritual abuse in a Christian faith setting or relationship, or perhaps you are exploring whether or not you have experienced such abuse, I wrote this book for you. This workbook is a resource for Christians who want to engage their spirituality and faith as a resource.

I write this primarily from the perspective of a professional counselor and spiritual-abuse researcher. But I want you to know that I am also a survivor of spiritual abuse. I will share a small portion of my story in this workbook.

Recommendations

I have a few recommendations as you begin this workbook.

This workbook is only one step in your healing process, not the entire journey. I provide tools, insight, and an opportunity to process your experiences. I consider this workbook a launching point for healing or a continuation of a journey you have already begun. Healing does not happen in twelve weeks. Healing is a process that looks different for every survivor. And it takes time. For me, it took years, and there are times it still hurts, like an old injury that flares up again if hit in a certain way.

I encourage you to join with others to go through this workbook. While you can go through this workbook alone, I encourage you to consider going through it with others. For example, you might try any of the following:

- Choose a few close friends who have experienced spiritual abuse and go through the book together.
- Find or start a support group.
- Work with a therapist.

You may choose to journey through this book by yourself. If you prefer that path, I encourage you to have a support system or the number of a counselor to call if you become overwhelmed. I provide a list of websites in the appendix that you can use to locate a counselor in your area.

You can go through the workbook at the pace that works for you. You are not in a race or competing with anyone; neither is your value based on completing any of these activities.

You can work with a professional mental-health provider as part of your healing journey. Consider engaging the help of a mental-health provider if you are experiencing any of the following:

- Emotional dysregulation that interferes with your daily functioning (see Week 1: Day 2 for a description and symptoms of emotional dysregulation). We will learn some tools for emotional dysregulation in this book, but if the tools do not work or if the dysregulation worsens, consider professional support.

- Intrusive thoughts or distressing images about the experience
- Increased anxiety, panic, or feeling constantly "on edge"
- Feelings of hopelessness
- Difficulty performing daily tasks
- Sleep disturbances
- Multiple forms of abuse. For example, some experience sexual abuse in the church in addition to spiritual abuse. Or, in the case of spiritual abuse in families, multiple other forms of abuse may have been present (i.e., physical, emotional, sexual). In that case, I recommend working with a professional counselor, as this could become dysregulating as you begin to process your experience.

Although spiritual abuse does not leave physical marks, please do not underestimate the harm it can cause.

Structure of Each Week

I follow a general structure, so you will know what to expect as you go through this workbook. I begin each week with some brief information about the week's topic, and you will have the opportunity to work through a different task each day. These are the components of each week:

- ❑ **Introduction.** I will overview the topic for the week.
- ❑ **Grounding.** I will provide you with a tool to assist you with grounding yourself to safety in the present moment. In the beginning, we will review the grounding skill on day 1. Beginning in week 4 and following, we will review grounding on day 2. I recommend you practice the new grounding tool all week. It is important you practice these daily, both when you need them and when you do not feel like you need them. You are building a toolbox of tools. By the end of this workbook, I hope you have an entire toolbox you can use. Of course, as with any toolbox, some tools will be more useful to you than others.

- ❑ **Your story.** We will explore your story of spiritual abuse and the holistic impact you experienced as a result.
- ❑ **Exploring thoughts and beliefs.** We will explore unhelpful thoughts or beliefs impacted by the spiritually abusive setting. Some of these unhelpful thoughts and beliefs are prevalent in society at large, so even if they were not part of your spiritually abusive experience, they may still apply.
- ❑ **Skills.** We will review some helpful skills for emotional, relational, and spiritual health and healing.
- ❑ **Holding hope.** We will explore some passages from the Bible that may bring hope and encouragement. Following are some of the topics I cover in Scripture:
  - ❍ The destructive nature of abusive practices
  - ❍ Jesus's teaching against abusive practices
  - ❍ How valuable you are and how much God loves you
  - ❍ The character of God contrasted with the spiritual abuser
  - ❍ God's mercy and forgiveness
  - ❍ Passages that display a range of emotions and lament
- ❑ **Primary takeaway.** Each week, I invite you to write your primary takeaway from the week. What impacted you the most?
- ❑ **Rest**. On the final day of each week, I invite you to choose a pleasurable activity and rest.

A Word about Healing

Healing is not linear. It's quite the opposite. I have placed topics at the beginning that are important foundational topics to consider. For example, before unpacking trauma, it is crucial to develop some tools for grounding because it can be emotionally and physically distressing when recalling traumatic events.

Additionally, healing looks different for everyone. For example, some survivors of spiritual abuse in a church setting choose to return to a church similar to their previous church and within the same denomination. In contrast, others prefer to attend a church of a different denomination or worship style. Others may join a Bible study in someone's home to build their sense of safety. There is no one-size-fits-all when it comes to healing.

Comfort Items

I recommend you gather some comfort items to have with you as you complete each day's activity. You can also use these items if you feel dysregulated during the week.

- ❏ A water bottle with ice-cold water
- ❏ An object of comfort—a soft blanket, a pillow, a robe, a pet, maybe even cozy clothes. Feel free to pick more than one.
- ❏ Something that smells calming to you. You might peruse the essential oils aisle at a local store and find a scent that feels calming and comforting, or choose a candle in a relaxing scent.
- ❏ Mints or gum
- ❏ Pens or pencils you enjoy using
- ❏ A fidget toy
- ❏ A location that feels reflective and calm (if possible)

Recommended Resources

In addition to your comfort items, I recommend the following resources:

- ❏ **The book *Understanding Spiritual Abuse: What It Is and How to Respond.***[1] I wrote this workbook for survivors of spiritual abuse to use as a supplement to the book.

[1] Karen Roudkovski, *Understanding Spiritual Abuse: What It Is and How to Respond* (Brentwood, TN: B&H Academic, 2024).

- ❑ **A Bible.** A study Bible would be helpful as you explore the passages I refer to and apply them to your life. You might also consider using **commentaries** as you explore Scripture for yourself.

A Word about Groups

If you are journeying through this with other survivors, there are "group norms" or expectations to consider. I include some group guidelines and a discussion guide in the appendix.

My Prayer for You

Heavenly Father,

I pray for these weary and hurting souls. That they may find rest in

your love,
your mercy,
your presence, and
your lovingkindness.

May you restore them, establish them, strengthen them, and support them as they seek healing.

In your merciful name, amen.

Week 1

WHAT IS SPIRITUAL ABUSE?

Welcome to week 1! You are brave for exploring your experience and considering what recovery and healing might look like. If you have not read the introduction, please do so now.

Our goals for the week (feel free to check off the boxes as you complete the goal):

- ❑ Focus of the week: Define *spiritual abuse*. Take the Spiritual Abuse Assessment.
- ❑ Grounding: Practice the 54321 grounding skill.
- ❑ Your story: Compare the definition of *spiritual abuse* to your situation.
- ❑ Explore thoughts and beliefs about trusting others.
- ❑ Skills: Describe and identify safe people.
- ❑ Holding hope: Share your cares and hurts with God.
- ❑ Recommended reading from *Understanding Spiritual Abuse*: If you are reading along in the book, you can read chapters 1 and 2 this week to explore a brief history of the term *spiritual abuse*, how it

may present in various settings, and information about the Spiritual Abuse Assessment.

Day 1: Introduction: What Is Spiritual Abuse?

When did you first hear the term *spiritual abuse*?

List some words or phrases that come to mind when you hear the term *spiritual abuse.*

Draw a picture of what image comes to mind when you think of the term *spiritual abuse.* Or, describe the image that comes to mind when you think of the term.

There is no universally agreed-upon definition of *spiritual abuse*, but here is the definition I propose based on previous descriptions and research:

> **a misuse of power in a spiritual context in which a person or group uses various coercive and manipulative methods of controlling the victim, resulting in the abused individual experiencing spiritual, emotional/psychological, physical, or relational harm.**[1]

[1] Karen Roudkovski, *Understanding Spiritual Abuse: What It Is and How to Respond* (Brentwood, TN: B&H Academic, 2024), 15.

On day 3, we will explore how this definition applies to your situation. Now, I invite you to take the Spiritual Abuse Assessment.

The Spiritual Abuse Assessment[2]

Instructions: Take a few moments to reflect on your spiritual and religious history in group settings and individual relationships.

With your spiritual and religious history in mind, has there been a time in your life when you had a negative or hurtful spiritual or religious experience as a result of an individual's or group's behavior? The experience may have been a single event or something you experienced over a period of time.

____ No, I do not recall a negative or hurtful spiritual or religious experience.
____ Yes, I do recall a negative or hurtful spiritual or religious experience.

If you have experienced more than one negative or hurtful spiritual experience, please answer the questions based on the most difficult experience. The questions are written in the past tense. If the negative or hurtful experience is still happening, please answer the questions as if they are written in the present tense.

Please answer the following questions based on your negative or hurtful experience.	Strongly Disagree	Disagree	Agree	Strongly Agree	Score
I was NOT permitted to make my own decisions without approval.	0	1	2	3	
My behavior was constantly being monitored.	0	1	2	3	

[2] Karen Roudkovski, *The Spiritual Abuse Assessment: A Tool for Survivors and Their Helpers* (Brentwood, TN: B&H Academic, 2024).

I had freedom to decline participation in an activity without fear of negative consequences.	0	1	2	3	
Obedience to the individual or group was required to avoid negative consequences.	0	1	2	3	
I was permitted to question the teachings of the individual or group without fear of retaliation.	0	1	2	3	
I was isolated from others outside the spiritual community or relationship.	0	1	2	3	
				Control Score:	
I feel damaged by the experience.	0	1	2	3	
I believe my personal spiritual needs were neglected.	0	1	2	3	
I experienced negative physical symptoms due to my negative spiritual experience.	0	1	2	3	
My spiritual needs were exploited in order for the individual(s) to maintain power and/or control.	0	1	2	3	
I was blamed for causing trouble when I questioned the actions or beliefs of the individual(s) in power.	0	1	2	3	
				Harm Score:	
(Add the control and harm scores to calculate your total scores.) Total Score:					

SCORING: A total score of 12 or higher indicates spiritual abuse.

Spiritual abuse exists on a spectrum of control and harm. Please graph your control, harm, and total scores below:

Control Score: Shade in all numbers up to and including the score on your assessment. Higher scores indicate increased areas of control.

7	8	9	10	11	12	13	14	15	16	17	18

Harm Score: Shade in all numbers up to and including the score on your assessment. Higher scores indicate higher incidences of harm.

6	7	8	9	10	11	12	13	14	15

Total Score: Shade in all numbers up to and including the score on your assessment. Higher scores indicate higher levels of spiritual abuse.

12–13	14–15	16–17	18–19	20–21	22–23	24–25	26–27	28–29	30–31	32–33

Important note: A lower score on the Spiritual Abuse Assessment does not necessarily mean you experience less impact than someone with a higher score. A complex combination of factors influences the effects of an abusive experience. Additionally, it is impossible to completely separate the areas of control and the areas of harm, so you will notice some overlap in these experiences.

As we conclude day 1, I encourage you to journal any concerns about completing this workbook in the space below. Do you have any hopes or goals through the process?

Day 2: Grounding: 54321

Thinking about your experience of spiritual abuse can be emotionally dysregulating. You may have a strong emotional response or even physical symptoms that feel difficult to contain. As you begin your healing journey, it is essential to develop tools to use if you become emotionally dysregulated or triggered. (We will explore the concept of triggers in week 3.)

We will refer to these tools as "grounding" tools. When we experience emotional dysregulation, we feel untethered or "ungrounded." Grounding tools can help bring you back to the present moment and regulate your nervous system when you feel overwhelmed.

You might experience the following symptoms if you are emotionally dysregulated:

- Increased heart rate
- Tightness in your chest or throat
- Feeling outside yourself
- Feeling detached from the present moment
- Stomach issues
- Feeling light-headed
- Intrusive, unwanted thoughts, memories, or "flashbacks"
- Difficulty focusing or concentrating
- Feeling "spaced out" or "dazed"
- Feeling "shut down" or withdrawn
- Feeling agitated
- Feeling panic
- Hypervigilant—feeling "on edge" and constantly appraising for danger in your environment
- Feeling "shut down"

The above symptoms can serve as signs that your nervous system, often referred to as your "fight, flight, freeze" response, is activated and needs regulation and soothing. If you experience any of these symptoms, you can use one or more grounding tools we will learn throughout this book to begin calming your nervous system. (See the appendix for a compiled list of the tools.) In week 3, we will add "pleasurable activities" so you have a broad array of coping skills for regular maintenance to cope with the stressors of daily living.

In the introduction, I recommended you pull together some comfort items to use while completing this workbook. If you have not yet gathered those items, I encourage you to do this today.

Grounding: 54321

The first tool for grounding is called "54321." You can use this tool when you feel emotionally dysregulated. The tools you will learn in this book are helpful in calming the "fight, flight, or freeze" sensations you experience. These tools are best rehearsed when you think you do not need them so they are more easily accessed when you do need them. When emotionally dysregulated, it is not easy to practice a new skill.

54321

- Describe 5 things you can see. (Use descriptive language. See the example below.)
- Describe 4 things you can touch. (Describe the texture.)
- Describe 3 things you can hear.
- Describe 2 things you can smell.
- Describe 1 thing you can taste. (I recommend having mints, minty or sour gum, sour candy, or ice-cold water available.)

Below is an example of this skill I am using while sitting on my sofa early in the morning.

- 5 things I can see: a tan sofa; green velvet curtains; a throw pillow with red, yellow, and blue flowers; white cabinets; and a gold lamp

- 4 things I can touch: a soft, fluffy blanket; the slightly rough surface of the sofa; the slick surface of my computer; and coarse threads of embroidery on the throw pillow
- 3 things I can hear: the refrigerator humming, birds chirping outside, and the keyboard clicking as I type
- 2 things I can smell: coffee brewing and pine and eucalyptus essential oil
- 1 thing I can taste: warm coffee with a touch of brown sugar creamer.

Practice this skill wherever you are sitting, then move outside or to another room and practice it again. Continue practicing this skill at least once daily when you feel like you do not need it, and practice it anytime you feel dysregulated.

I recommend you consider posting these grounding skills somewhere you can see them, such as on your desk or the refrigerator. Or, you can write your favorite on index "coping cards." You can also store them on your phone, even using them as your phone background.

Day 3: Your Story: Applying the Definition of Spiritual Abuse

I introduced the definition of *spiritual abuse* on day 1. Now, we are going to apply it to your spiritually abusive experience.

Spiritual abuse is "**a misuse of power in a spiritual context in which a person or group** uses various coercive and manipulative methods of controlling the victim, resulting in the abused individual experiencing spiritual, emotional/psychological, physical, or relational harm."[3]

---

[3] Roudkovski, *Understanding Spiritual Abuse*, 15.

This week, we will focus on the first phrase, "a misuse of power in a spiritual context in which a person or group . . ."

"Misuse of power": Spiritual abuse occurs when there is a power imbalance. Think of this as actual power, not perceived power. Spiritual abuse is most commonly recognized when a minister spiritually abuses a congregant. However, research indicates that ministers or other leaders may be the victims of spiritual abuse when another person or group holds the power. If a minister has spiritually abused you, this may not be easy to read. If you are a minister who experienced spiritual abuse, you may feel great relief at this acknowledgment.

Describe the power imbalance in your situation:

"A spiritual context": Spiritual abuse requires a spiritual context, but the context does not have to be a church or other formal religious setting. It can be any spiritual or religious setting. Spiritual abuse can occur in a variety of religions, denominations, parachurch organizations, religious schools, and spiritual centers. Spiritual abuse may occur in a variety of relationships, such as marriage, parenting, mentorship, or discipleship.

➢ What was the context of your spiritually abusive situation?

"A person or group": Spiritual abuse may be perpetrated by a single individual or a group of individuals.

➢ Were you spiritually abused by a group or an individual? Or both?

"Uses various coercive and manipulative methods of controlling the victim": We will explore methods of control in weeks 6 and 7. You will have the opportunity to apply the information to your experience.

"Resulting in the abused individual experiencing spiritual, emotional/psychological, physical, or relational harm": We will explore and consider your experience of harm in week 8.

Please take a few moments to notice how you are doing right now as we begin exploring your spiritually abusive situation.

What emotions are you noticing? (An emotion chart is located in the appendix.)

What physical sensations are coming up for you?

What thoughts are you having?

Practice your 54321 grounding skill to help calm any dysregulation you may feel.

Day 4: Exploring Thoughts and Beliefs about Trust

Each week, we will explore some unhelpful or untrue thoughts and beliefs that can develop during a spiritually abusive experience. Some will apply to you, while others may not.

At first, you may experience great difficulty noticing and changing these beliefs. You are forging new pathways in your brain, so this is expected.

Let me illustrate. I grew up in the foothills of the Smoky Mountains in East Tennessee. Countless hiking paths wind through those mountains, coves, and valleys. Imagine we are beginning a hike into the thick, dense forest of the Smokies. You start toward the well-worn hiking trail, but I stop you and request that you forge a new path with me where there is currently no path. The well-traveled path is easy. Creating a new way through the overgrown brush and limbs will be challenging. But, if we continue to use the new path, it will get easier.

Changing your thoughts and beliefs and learning new tools, such as your new grounding tools, requires effort and repetition. Reverting to the old pathway comes more quickly and is more accessible. It is well-worn. But, over time, the new path will become worn and easier to use. Eventually, the old pathway will become overgrown and less natural to use. This concept of forging a new path is why practicing your grounding tools is essential.

Persistent Practice Is the Key to New Pathways

It takes time to forge a new path, so be patient with yourself. Think of the dense forest and what it might be like to create a new path in the forest. Time, effort, desire, and determination are required.

Trust

Turning to our first set of unhelpful thoughts and beliefs, we will examine the concept of "trust."

Spiritual abusers misuse and misrepresent the name of God and Scripture or theological teachings to gain and maintain control of the abused. As a result, trust is impacted. Unhelpful and untrue beliefs and thoughts about trusting God and others may develop.

These might include the following beliefs: (I left space for you to add your own.)

- ➢ I cannot trust others.
- ➢ I cannot trust God to ________________________________.

- I cannot trust myself.
- I cannot trust myself to make good decisions about others.
- I am alone.
- ____

Ask yourself, What would I like to believe instead? (Add your ideas.)

- ❑ I can make good decisions about trusting others.
- ❑ I can take it slow in getting to know others.
- ❑ ____
- ❑ ____

Throughout this workbook, we will identify and challenge unhelpful thoughts. Because of the nature of a traumatic experience, you may find it exceptionally difficult to "think" your way out of these thoughts, particularly when emotionally dysregulated. In those times, ground yourself using your tools and recognize this is a trauma response. Trauma therapies, such as EMDR (eye movement desensitization and reprocessing), can assist with processing the trauma.

You may have noticed that I provided a thought log at the back of this workbook. Do not be concerned about using that yet. We will cover the various parts of the thought log over the next few weeks. When we finish reviewing the features of the log, you will be able to complete a log in week 4.

Consider an example of an unhelpful thought you experienced related to trusting others and complete the following:

Name your thought(s).

On a scale of 0 to 100 percent, how true do you believe this thought to be?

What are some alternative ways of thinking about this situation? What is a more helpful thought?

How true do you believe the helpful thought to be? (0–100 percent)

Begin noticing your thoughts. Be curious. Find alternative ways to think when needed. We will continue this "thought noticing" journey for the remainder of the workbook.

Day 5: Skills: Safe People

In *Understanding Spiritual Abuse*, I describe what safe spiritual communities look like. We will explore safe communities in the final week. But this week, we will focus on individual relationships. For today's skill, let's explore the concept of safe people:

- Safe people are dependable, honest, and trustworthy. They avoid gossiping to others about you. Are they gossiping to you about others? Be cautious if this is happening.
- Safe people have personal boundaries and encourage you to have healthy boundaries. They respect the boundaries you set. (We will discuss boundaries in week 3.)
- Safe people believe that your acceptance is not based on your performance. It is not earned.
- Safe people accept disagreement and questions. And, while they may not always agree with you, they treat you respectfully. If you raise a concern, they are non-defensive.
- Safe people provide kind but direct communication. You are encouraged to practice open and direct communication as well.

- Safe people respond with empathy when you communicate with them. Empathy is the ability to take a non-defensive, curious posture of trying to understand what another person is experiencing rather than quickly rushing to judgment or trying to "fix" a person.
- Are there any other qualities that are important to you?

  ____

Trust takes time, especially if you experienced betrayal and hurt in a relationship that you expected to be safe. Look for the qualities listed above. Allow time to pass as you begin to build trust little by little.

The Process of Building Trust

Think of building trust like how you would safely swim in an unknown lake. You could dive into the lake in the middle of the night, jumping in head first without thinking of the depth and temperature or what was swimming below. However, that would be risky and potentially dangerous. The more cautious course of action is to first go in the daylight. Look around. Are others swimming safely? Perhaps you prefer clarity in the water to observe what might be swimming below. Maybe you dip your toe in to check the temperature. Then, you slowly wade forward, cautious of steep drops or other potential dangers.

Similarly, you can cautiously dip your toe into a new relationship. Perhaps you begin with a cup of coffee and a conversation. Look for signs that they are safe. You are free to get to know someone over time.

Think of a person from somewhere in your past who felt safe. Describe what made that person safe.

Think about your current relationships. Can you name a safe person?

____

- Describe the characteristics that make that person feel safe.

- Describe a time when that individual demonstrated their trustworthiness.

- If you cannot think of anyone, describe the characteristics you are looking for and where you might meet someone similar to this description.

- If you cannot think of a safe person, this may indicate you could benefit from a professional counselor to journey with you as you walk through your story.

Important: I want to stress that if we trust and become vulnerable with another person, we open ourselves up to hurt. We cannot avoid this. Even safe people are not perfect people and can say or do something hurtful. Look for patterns. Is the behavior a pattern? What happens when you tell the person their comment or behavior hurt you?

Not everyone in your life will have the same level of trust. We will use the concept of a house to illustrate how you might trust and feel safe with a person at varying levels. You can think of this imagery as you build relationships and "test the waters" of whether or not a person is safe and trustworthy.

The house you live in has doors that serve a purpose. We are in control of who enters our home. Some of you also have a fence around your house. If not, for this exercise, imagine you have a gate or fence in front of your home. You can have visitors at any of the places in your home listed below. People can move from a place of less trust to a place of more trust or vice versa. The further we go into your home, the more we will illustrate the increased safety and trust of the individual.

- ❏ **Outside the gate**. Some individuals have not yet earned your trust or have proven unsafe. You can imagine them outside your gate of trust. You can chat with them across the fence while you see if you might want to invite them to your porch.
- ❏ **On the front porch**. A front porch is comfortable and a great place to get to know someone. You can chat on the front porch without inviting someone into your home.
- ❏ **In the living room**. Next, you might invite someone into your home through the front door and into the living room. Imagine this as a living room that is not open to your entire home but is separate. There is still a separation, but trust is building.
- ❏ **In your kitchen**. Imagine you have invited someone into your kitchen. This room indicates that you trust the person. Your closest friends and family can come in this space, but not everyone has earned the trust to be here.

Are there any individuals you want to invite to your front porch?

Or perhaps someone has been outside your gate or on the front porch whom you would like to invite inside? What characteristics does that person exhibit that encourage you to ask them onto the porch so you can get to know them better?

Is there a time this week you might spend with this person or make some form of contact? Write your plan in this space.

Who is in your kitchen? Do you need time with them as you proceed through this workbook?

Day 6: Holding Hope in God's Love

In this workbook, we begin our Scripture exploration by reminding ourselves how the Bible emphasizes and describes love. I invite you to read 1 Corinthians 13:1–13:

> If I speak human or angelic tongues but do not have love, I am a noisy gong or a clanging cymbal. If I have the gift of prophecy and understand all mysteries and all knowledge, and if I have all faith so that I can move mountains but do not have love, I am nothing. And if I give away all my possessions, and if I give over my body in order to boast but do not have love, I gain nothing.
>
> Love is patient, love is kind. Love does not envy, is not boastful, is not arrogant, is not rude, is not self-seeking, is not irritable, and does not keep a record of wrongs. Love finds no joy in unrighteousness but rejoices in the truth. It bears all things, believes all things, hopes all things, endures all things.
>
> Love never ends. But as for prophecies, they will come to an end; as for tongues, they will cease; as for knowledge, it will come to an end. For we know in part, and we prophesy in part, but when the perfect comes, the partial will come to an end. When I was a child, I spoke like a child, I thought like a child, I reasoned like a

> child. When I became a man, I put aside childish things. For now we see only a reflection as in a mirror, but then face to face. Now I know in part, but then I will know fully, as I am fully known. Now these three remain: faith, hope, and love—but the greatest of these is love.

Underline the words and phrases in the passage above that describe those who do *not* have love.

Circle the words and phrases that describe those who *do* have love.

How can we apply this description of love to the actions and attitudes of safe people?

Do you want to add anything to our description of safe people based on your reading of this passage?

As we journey through this workbook, keep in mind that the actions and attitudes of spiritual abusers do not reflect God's intention for our relationships.

We will conclude today by reading John 3:16–17, where we see the greatest expression of God's love for us.

> For God loved the world in this way: He gave his one and only Son, so that everyone who believes in him will not perish but have eternal life. For God did not send his Son into the world to condemn the world, but to save the world through him.

Day 7: Rest

After being in an atmosphere of performance-based acceptance, some of you may have difficulty allowing yourself to rest. You may even experience feelings of anxiety, restlessness, or guilt. For others, you may be relieved that someone is telling you to rest. You can refer to this day as your sabbath or your day of rest. I invite you to do a pleasurable activity on your day of rest. Which pleasurable activity do you choose today?

Week 1: Primary Takeaway

What is your primary takeaway from this week?

Week 2

EMOTIONS MATTER

Welcome to week 2! This week is all about emotions.

Our goals for the week:

- ❏ Focus of the week: Emotions. What are they? Why do we have them?
- ❏ Grounding: Learn how to take the temperature of your emotions with the "emotional thermometer."
- ❏ Your story: Identify some messages about emotions communicated through your life.
- ❏ Explore thoughts and beliefs about emotions.
- ❏ Skills: Pleasurable activities
- ❏ Holding hope: Exploring the emotions in Psalm 142, "a cry of distress"
- ❏ Recommended reading from *Understanding Spiritual Abuse*: Read chapter 6 for a brief section on emotions contained within a discussion on the importance of responding well to disclosures of spiritual abuse so the response does not further traumatize the survivor.

Day 1: Emotions

As a professional counselor, I have heard countless misconceptions about emotions. I have observed the concern that emotions, if acknowledged, might become overwhelming. I have seen attempts to avoid emotions, with the avoidance eventually resulting in some significant emotional, relational, and physical challenges. Emotions will surface one way or another, even by way of physical symptoms.

Because emotions are such an impactful and vital part of our lives, I want to provide an opportunity to explore the concept of emotions. Here are some truths about emotions:

- ❏ God created emotions. His creation is good.
- ❏ In Scripture, we see God displaying emotion.
- ❏ Jesus exhibited emotion.
- ❏ Emotions have a purpose.
- ❏ Emotions provide information.

Emotions are like the warning light on our vehicles. Would you ignore the check engine light on your car? No. Disregarding a check engine light could be costly. Emotions, like warning lights, indicate we need to look below the surface. We need to be curious and investigate what they might be telling us.

Work through the following emotion activity:

- ➢ Turn to the emotion chart in the appendix.
- ➢ Name the emotion(s) you are noticing. When naming emotions, it is best to use more detailed descriptive words than the less helpful "good," "bad," "sad," and "mad."
- ➢ Notice where you are experiencing the emotion in your body.

- If the emotion is difficult or dysregulating, ride the wave of the emotion. Ground yourself using your coping strategies. Say a truthful statement to yourself:
  - This, too, shall pass.
  - I can ride this wave of emotion until it passes.
  - What I am feeling is old stuff bubbling to the surface.
  - This feeling will not last forever.
  - I am okay.
  - I can survive this.
  - It's okay to feel ______.
  - These feelings are painful, but they will eventually pass.
  - I can use my grounding and coping skills.
  - I can notice what this feeling is conveying.
  - I can be curious about the feeling.
  - ______________________________
  - ______________________________
- Be curious. Ask yourself,
  - What information is this emotion providing?
  - What thoughts are accompanying the emotion?
  - What occurred in the past twenty-four hours that may have contributed to how I feel now?
  - Could this be related to any difficulty or traumatic event from the past?
- Ask yourself:
  - Is there an action to be taken based on this information?
  - Is there a boundary I need to set?
  - Is there an indication I need to take care of my body (e.g., sleep, hydration, nutrition)?

Day 2: Grounding: Taking Your Temperature

As I write this workbook, we are enjoying the summer season turning to fall. In South Louisiana, our summers are hot and humid, but this particular summer, we had even higher temperatures and humidity than usual. Temperature extremes, whether hot or cold, can be uncomfortable. And, at times, downright miserable.

Let's imagine your emotional temperature similarly. You have a "comfortable" range. You also have a "too hot" or "too cold" range. We will envision this as a thermometer. As the temperature rises, you may experience physical symptoms, such as an increased heart rate, tightness in your chest, a clenched jaw, or a swirly stomach. You may feel disconnected, withdrawn, shut down, or numb if the temperature gets too low.

Both temperature extremes indicate distress. With both, you might experience physical symptoms similar to those experienced when you feel anxious or fearful. Distress is a whole-body experience, not limited to thoughts. Even though we do not always make the connection, we feel distress throughout our bodies.

A headache, a clenched jaw, tense shoulders, a tight throat, a flutter in our chest, and a nauseous stomach can all be symptoms of emotional distress. You might withdraw or have a "short fuse." Notice how distress impacts you.

Describe how it feels to be in your ideal temperature range.

What are signs you are getting "too hot" (e.g., feeling anxious, sweaty palms, increased heart rate, irritable)?

Where do you experience this in your body?

What thoughts go through your mind in these moments?

What behaviors do you exhibit when you are getting "too hot"?

What are signs you are getting "too cold" (e.g., shutting down, avoidance, difficulty with motivation)?

Where do you experience this in your body?

What thoughts go through your mind in these moments?

What behaviors do you exhibit when you are getting "too cold"?

Have you experienced either of these in the past week? If so, describe the experience.

Spend the next few days noticing your temperature. Observe when your temperature gets out of your comfort zone. Consider the following when you see you are becoming dysregulated and your temperature is getting too high or too low:

- Name what emotions you are experiencing and how those emotions feel in your body.
- What happened just before the temperature change? What happened during the previous twenty-four hours?
- Notice what you tell yourself.
- Observe what actions you take.
- When you experience the temperature moving to either extreme, that is a sign to engage your grounding skills. Ground yourself to the present moment. Breathe.
- Be curious about what turned the temperature up or down.
- What pleasurable activities can you use to self-soothe and calm? See the appendix for some ideas. Try grounding or a pleasurable activity the next time you notice your temperature moving out of the comfortable range.

We will revisit your emotional-temperature observations next week, so you might find it helpful to take a few notes or journal about what you notice this week.

Day 3: Your Story: Messages about Emotions

Throughout our lives, we receive messages about emotions. These messages can come from our parents, our church, our friends, our culture, and from the spiritually abusive settings in which we find ourselves.

Some of you may have grown up in a spiritually abusive home, so the exploration of childhood messages and spiritual-abuser messages will intersect in this activity.

If you find this dysregulating, remember you can stop anytime. Take a break. Practice grounding. Then, reevaluate if this is something you want to pursue on your own or if you want to find a professional to walk alongside you in this journey.

What were you taught about emotions when you were a child?

As a child, what happened when you cried? How did your caregivers respond?

As a child, what happened when you were angry? How did your caregivers respond?

In the spiritually abusive situation, what were you taught about emotions?

In the spiritually abusive situation, did you ever exhibit a difficult emotion (e.g., sadness, grief, anger)? If so, what was the response?

In spiritually abusive relationships or settings, emotions may have been

- **Overemphasized or minimized:** Positive emotions may have been celebrated (overemphasized), while difficult emotions may have been viewed as spiritual immaturity (minimized).
- **Used to manipulate:** The emotions of fear, guilt, and shame are often used to manipulate because these are powerful emotions that most of us would rather avoid feeling.

If applicable, how were emotions overemphasized or minimized in your spiritually abusive situation?

How were emotions used to manipulate in your spiritually abusive situation?

Tomorrow, we will explore your beliefs about emotions. Today, though, I invite you to practice your 54321 grounding tool, then continue doing so as needed as you move through this workbook.

Day 4: Exploring Thoughts and Beliefs about Emotions

Continuing with our exploration of messages you received both in your childhood and in the spiritually abusive relationship, let's explore what beliefs you developed about emotion.

Do any of the following statements reflect your current belief (or what you believed previously)?

- Emotions (or feelings) are not important.
- Emotional needs are not important.
- Ignore your emotions.
- Feeling emotion is a sign of weakness or spiritual immaturity.
- I need to wear a "mask" so others do not see my emotions.
- Emotions are either "good" or "bad."
- Any others? ______________________________

What are more helpful beliefs about emotions?

- Emotions are important.
- Emotions provide information.
- My emotional needs matter.
- I can notice my emotions with curiosity.
- Feeling and experiencing emotion requires bravery and maturity.
- I can be honest with myself about my emotions.
- Any others? ___________________________________

One common issue I encounter as a mental-health provider is individuals who experience guilt or shame over experiencing certain emotions. Countless times, I have been asked, "Is it wrong to feel ________?" Let's reframe this question. Instead, be curious and ask yourself, "What information is this emotion providing me?"

What emotions do you see God expressing in Scripture?

What emotions do you see Jesus expressing in Scripture?

What emotions do you feel in response to your experience of spiritual abuse? (See the emotion chart in the appendix.)

Based on what we have discussed in this chapter, what would you say to a friend who asked you if it was wrong to feel a particular emotion?

Day 5: Skills: Pleasurable Activities

Part of healing is allowing yourself to do pleasurable activities. If you have been in a spiritually abusive relationship or group, you may have difficulty remembering what you enjoy doing just for fun. You may feel guilty when you engage in anything playful. This response is normal, but I encourage you to develop your repertoire of pleasurable activities. Acknowledge any feelings of guilt, but do not allow them to prevent you from proceeding.

Let's brainstorm some "fun" or "play" activities here. I included a list of ideas in the appendix to get you started.

What do you enjoy doing in your free time?

What did you enjoy when you were a child or teen?

Is there something you have always wanted to try? List it here. Feel free to add multiple ideas. No idea is too simple. The simple things in life are often the best, aren't they?

Choose one of the pleasurable activities and do it today. Write your choice in the space below.

Begin incorporating a pleasurable activity each day. It can be as simple as eating lunch outside, having a warm mug of tea while looking out the window, or playing with your pet.

Day 6: Holding Hope: The Psalms

Sadness. Despair. Joy. Hope. The book of Psalms is replete with emotion, vulnerable expression, and raw honesty. In the CSB, Psalm 142 is entitled "A Cry of Distress." Underline the words and phrases that describe David's emotional state and his distress.

> I cry aloud to the LORD;
> I plead aloud to the LORD for mercy.
> I pour out my complaint before him;
> I reveal my trouble to him.
> Although my spirit is weak within me,
> you know my way.
> Along this path I travel
> they have hidden a trap for me.
> Look to the right and see:
> no one stands up for me;
> there is no refuge for me;
> no one cares about me.
> I cry to you, LORD;
> I say, "You are my shelter,
> my portion in the land of the living."
> Listen to my cry,
> for I am very weak.
> Rescue me from those who pursue me,

for they are too strong for me.
Free me from prison
so that I can praise your name.
The righteous will gather around me
because you deal generously with me.

Use this space to journal how you relate to the descriptions in this psalm.

What requests does the author make to God?

What are your requests?

Day 7: Rest

Which pleasurable activity do you choose?

Week 2: Primary Takeaway

What is your primary takeaway from this week?

Week 3

SAFETY AND IDENTIFYING TRIGGERS

This week, we will briefly explore the impact of trauma and how you can continue establishing a sense of safety.

Our goals for the week:

- ❏ Focus of the week: Establishing safety and considering the question, "Do I stay or do I go?"
- ❏ Grounding: Peaceful place
- ❏ Your story: Identifying triggers
- ❏ Exploring thoughts and beliefs about safety
- ❏ Skills: Setting boundaries
- ❏ Holding hope in the names and descriptions of God seen in Scripture
- ❏ Recommended reading from *Understanding Spiritual Abuse*: I briefly discuss the concept of triggers in chapter 7, "Treatment Considerations."

Day 1: Do I Stay or Do I Go?

Some of you reading this workbook have left the spiritually abusive setting, while others may still be in the spiritually abusive relationship or environment. If you are currently in a spiritually abusive setting, you are faced with the choice to stay or leave. Either option comes with a cost.

If you leave, you might lose relationships or face rejection. You could be labeled a "troublemaker" or experience attacks on your reputation or personhood.

If you left the spiritually abusive situation, describe any repercussions or harm you experienced as a result.

Some people choose to stay in an attempt to bring about change. Staying comes with an even greater potential cost. If that is where you find yourself, consider the following questions:

- Is there anyone to report to who will listen and help bring about change?
- Can you be emotionally, physically, spiritually, and relationally healthy if you stay?
- Who is your support system?
- How long are you willing to stay? What boundaries do you need to set? Will those boundaries be respected?
- How will you know it is time to go?
- What are your expectations if you stay? Make these as specific as possible to evaluate how likely you believe these are to happen.
- On a scale from 1 (not likely at all) to 10 (very likely), how likely is it that your expectations will be met?

Whether you stay or leave, you may experience triggers of the traumatic experience that seem to take you right back to the initial experience itself. We will explore the concept of triggers on day 3.

Day 2: Grounding: Peaceful Place

Our grounding tool is called "peaceful place." Read through the directions and then practice the skill. Using this tool can take some practice, so do not give up if it initially feels awkward.

- Wherever you are, sit as comfortably as possible.
- Close your eyes or let your gaze gently settle on the ground before you.
- Take a few deep breaths, settling into the breathing rhythm that feels comfortable for your body.
- Think of a place that feels peaceful. It could be somewhere you have visited before or would like to visit one day, or perhaps it is a place you have seen on television or read about in a book and you imagine it to be quite beautiful and serene. Allow this to be a place that does not hold any negative memories or that you associate with a person or event that brings up negative thoughts or difficult emotions. For example, some choose a beach, mountain, or beside a waterfall or lake.
- Allow yourself to settle in the place in your mind. Look around. Imagine yourself finding a comfortable place to sit and relax. Add a comfortable chair or hammock if you desire.
- Now, let's engage the five senses.
- Look around and notice what you are seeing. What are the colors? Are there birds or other animals nearby? What is the landscape?
- Now, take a deep breath and notice what you smell. If you are at the beach, you may smell the salty air; in the mountains, you may smell the crisp fragrance of the leaves.

- ➢ Next, listen. What sounds do you hear? Birds chirping? The sound of water? Rustling leaves?
- ➢ As we engage the sense of feel and touch, imagine yourself touching the ground with your bare feet or wrapping a cozy blanket around you. Notice the temperature of the air. Is there a breeze blowing?
- ➢ Immerse yourself in the peacefulness and beauty. Notice your breath. Maintain this imagery for five minutes if possible.
- ➢ If distracting thoughts enter, notice them and let them float by with the breeze.

You can practice this skill daily before bedtime as you relax for the evening. You might notice some discomfort as you begin to sit quietly, especially if you have never done so before.

Day 3: Your Story: Identifying Triggers

Last week, we discussed how your "emotional temperature" might rise or fall, indicating you are in a place of emotional dysregulation. As you became aware of your "emotional temperature" over the past week, you may have noticed certain situations or triggers that made this temperature change to an uncomfortable level. Because spiritual abuse is considered a potentially traumatic event, events or objects that remind you of the abusive situation can be trauma triggers.

Perhaps you have heard the term *triggered*. When we use the word *trigger* in this workbook, it is an indication of the seriousness of spiritual abuse. A trigger refers to any situation or object that sets in motion a connection to an emotionally charged or traumatic event that a person experienced in their past. As a result, the survivor may have a physical response, emotional response, or intrusive thoughts or memories about the experience. You might feel your heart pounding, tightness in your chest, or a sick stomach. You might feel emotionally overwhelmed. You might have intrusive flashbacks of the event. Or, you may feel disconnected, outside of yourself, or as though you are shutting down. Sound familiar? These are the symptoms of emotional dysregulation we identified in weeks 1 and 2.

To first illustrate the concept of a trigger, I want you to think back to something slightly embarrassing and emotionally charged but not overwhelming or something you would consider traumatic. I believe all of us have those in the past. I'll share one of mine as an example. One Sunday, in my late teens, I substituted for the organ player at a nearby church. When I sat at the organ bench, I noticed it was wobbly, but by the end of the service, I had forgotten about the wobbly legs. I was playing the final song as the pastor prayed the closing prayer. During this solemn time, the bench tipped forward, launching me onto the keyboard. A horrific sound blared across the sanctuary. And, if you are familiar with an organ, you have probably already realized that when I tried to stand to catch my balance, my feet landed on the pedal board keys, adding to the ear-ringing chaos. At this point, you may be feeling secondhand embarrassment for me. I laugh every time I think about it. But, even after all this time and the humor I find in it, I still feel a slight embarrassment and discomfort for my mortified teenage self. I can almost feel my cheeks flush as I type this for you to read.

Now it's your turn to think back to something minimally embarrassing. Maybe close your eyes and imagine yourself there. Can you envision it in your mind? Now, I want you to notice any body sensations you are feeling. Isn't it amazing that we do not simply remember the event cognitively, but our body also remembers? This concept is particularly pertinent when we have experienced an event accompanied by elevated emotions.

Let's now apply this to memories of spiritual abuse. Because of the way memories work, spiritual experiences or spiritual symbols can become a trauma trigger. In my own experience, there were multiple triggers, but the two that were the most problematic in my healing journey were candles used in church and specific passages of Scripture. Anytime either of these would come up, my heart would race, and panic would rise. EMDR therapy (eye movement desensitization and reprocessing therapy) was helpful for me in processing these traumatic memories so certain Scriptures and candles in church no longer cause panic. (See the recommended resources at the end of this workbook for the website link to learn more about EMDR therapy and find a provider in your area.)

Have you noticed any triggers of your spiritually abusive situation? I listed some below and left space for you to describe and add your own.

- ❑ Bible verses or passages ______________________
- ❑ Song(s) ______________________
- ❑ Religious phrases ______________________
- ❑ Religious symbols ______________________
- ❑ Certain types of religious services or meetings ______________________
- ❑ Religious sacraments ______________________
- ❑ ______________________
- ❑ ______________________

Now let's combine the two topics we discussed this week. If you choose to stay in the spiritually abusive situation, how often are you feeling triggered?

Thinking about triggers is tough, and you may be feeling dysregulated. Please take the time to ground yourself back to the present moment. Practice your 54321 skill or peaceful place. Or, go to the appendix and choose a pleasurable activity for the next fifteen minutes. After fifteen minutes, evaluate how you are feeling. Use additional grounding or coping strategies as needed. Or, perhaps this might be a good time to call a support person to check in.

Day 4: Exploring Thoughts and Beliefs about Safety

Multiple factors contribute to a survivor of spiritual abuse feeling unsafe, powerless, or helpless. Spiritual abuse impacts our beliefs about safety. You may notice the following thoughts or beliefs:

- "I am powerless."
- "I am helpless."
- "I am not safe."
- Fill in your own: ______________________________

What do you want to believe about yourself instead?

- "I have choices."
- "I am capable."
- ______________________________

Due to the nature of trauma, it is common for survivors to feel unsafe even though they cognitively know that they are safe in the present moment. Begin observing times you feel safe or at peace. Continue practicing your grounding tools and pleasurable activities.

Think of an example of an unhelpful thought you experienced about your safety or feeling powerless and complete the following:

Name your thought(s).

On a scale of 0 to 100 percent, how true do you believe this thought to be?

What are some alternative ways of thinking about this situation? What is a more helpful thought?

How true do you believe the helpful thought to be? (0–100 percent)

When you feel powerless, it is helpful to determine what boundaries you may need to set. We will explore setting boundaries tomorrow.

Day 5: Skills: Setting Boundaries

Setting healthy boundaries is a beneficial skill. But it can feel highly unsafe to set boundaries, particularly if one has had a negative experience setting boundaries in the past—which is often the case for spiritual-abuse survivors. We will begin by exploring the purpose of boundaries, and you will start identifying some boundaries you want to set.

Boundaries:

- Differentiate us from others
- Allow us to set limits
- Are necessary for our emotional, spiritual, and physical well-being
- Are essential in healthy relationships

Boundaries are set with ourselves and with others. For example, you might place a boundary for yourself that you will only use social media for a certain number of minutes per week or take a break from social media for at least one day per week.

A boundary you set with both yourself and others might be avoiding gossip. Avoiding gossip requires a personal boundary and speaking up if the other person begins to share gossip.

A boundary set with others may be telling your child's school that you can volunteer twice monthly but not weekly. You might say, "I am happy to help with such an important need. I am available two times per month."

What are some boundaries we can set?

- ❑ Our time
- ❑ Our privacy (how much you choose to share with others)
- ❑ How much access people have to our lives and our resources
- ❑ Our speech (e.g., avoiding gossip)
- ❑ Financial boundaries (e.g., avoiding overspending)
- ❑ Protection of ourselves (emotionally, spiritually, and physically)
- ❑ Our willingness to stay in a harmful situation. For example, we cannot control how another person speaks to us, but we can control our response. We can choose to leave the situation. We can say, "We can discuss this when you can communicate without raising your voice."
- ❑ List any others you want to add: ____________________________

In a spiritually abusive situation, boundaries are often discouraged or disallowed. Or, if a person attempts to set a boundary, it is not respected. For example, these boundaries may include how you spend your time or other resources. Or, they might be an invasion of your privacy or unrealistic expectations. A boundary violation in a spiritually abusive setting might look like the demand to protect the institution over protecting an individual.

In the spiritually abusive relationship, what boundaries were violated?

Did you attempt to speak up and address the boundary violation? If so, what happened? If not, what were your concerns?

What boundaries do you want to set that would most impact your life now?

Look back at your list and choose one boundary that feels manageable to set. Name it below. Write out what you plan to do, and work on that this week.

Day 6: Holding Hope in the Refuge of God

When experiencing triggers, we feel unsafe. When those triggers are religious symbols or events, we may experience difficulty engaging in religious practices or attending church services. If Scripture was used to manipulate or justify the spiritual abuse, then specific passages may be particularly challenging. When the triggers involve the image of God, the situation becomes even more complex. Today, we will review a few images and names of God in Scripture that exhibit God's grace, lovingkindness, and long-suffering.

Circle the names or descriptions of God in the following passages:

The Lord is my rock, my fortress, and my deliverer,
my God, my rock where I seek refuge.
My shield, the horn of my salvation, my stronghold, my refuge,
and my Savior, you save me from violence. (2 Samuel 22:2–3)

I am at rest in God alone;
my salvation comes from him.
He alone is my rock and my salvation,
my stronghold; I will never be shaken. (Psalm 62:1–2)

He will cover you with his feathers;
you will take refuge under his wings.
His faithfulness will be a protective shield. (Psalm 91:4)

You are my shelter and my shield;
I put my hope in your word. (Psalm 119:114)

The name of the Lord is a strong tower;
the righteous run to it and are protected. (Proverbs 18:10)

The spiritual abuser may have presented themselves as some form of refuge or shelter, but there was no safety in that shelter. If that occurred, you may find it difficult to relate to these images as a safe place. If so, is there an image of God that feels safe to you?

Suppose you are currently experiencing triggers related to your faith. How might your life be different if your image of God was like the passages above rather than the image presented by the spiritual abuser?

Day 7: Rest

Which pleasurable activity do you choose?

Recommended Reading about Boundaries

Cloud, Henry, and John Townsend. *Boundaries*. Grand Rapids: Zondervan, 2017.

Week 3: Primary Takeaway

What is your primary takeaway from this week?

Week 4

CAUGHT IN A WEB (PART 1)

Have you ever walked into a spider web? Spider webs are difficult to notice before we step into them. And once we are caught in them, they are tough to escape as we remove thread after thread from our bodies. When we think we have finally removed the web, we find a stray piece.

Getting caught in a spiritually abusive situation is much like getting caught in a spider web: difficult to see coming and even more difficult to escape.

In the book *Understanding Spiritual Abuse*, I describe how the abuser entraps the victims in the web of spiritual abuse. For the next two weeks, we will explore how the abuser spins a web.

Our goals for the week:

- ❑ Focus of the week: Exploring the web of spiritual abuse
- ❑ Grounding: 478 breathing
- ❑ Your story: Exploring how you were caught in the web of spiritual abuse
- ❑ Exploring thoughts and beliefs about God
- ❑ Skills: Identifying unhelpful thinking patterns (Part 1)

- ❑ Holding hope: Contrasting the actions and attitudes of the spiritual abuser with that of Christ
- ❑ Recommended reading from *Understanding Spiritual Abuse*: In chapter 3 of *Understanding Spiritual Abuse*, I explore ways the abuser spins a web of control. Both research and Scripture reflect these practices. In this workbook, we will briefly overview eight of those ways. I highly recommend you read chapter 3 of the book for further descriptions and scriptural application from Matthew 23.

Day 1: Caught in a Web and Grounding

At some point in this journey, you may have asked yourself, "How did this happen to me? How did I get caught up in a spiritually abusive situation?" No one intends to enter a spiritually abusive situation. We are tangled in the web before we realize its presence. This week and next, we will explore how spiritual abusers entrap their victims.

Today, we will overview four of the ways spiritual abusers entrap, and on days 4 and 5, you will reflect on how they occurred in your life. Because each experience is different, you may find that not all areas apply to your situation.

1. *A "good" beginning.* Spiritually abusive situations typically begin positively and meet a need. Perhaps you were looking for a Christian community, spiritual growth, or a place to serve others. Maybe you were engaged by a charismatic pastor. You may have felt a sense of purpose and meaning.
2. *Self-appointed "divine" authority.* The spiritual abuser presents him- or herself as having a special or "divine" authority that ultimately begins to replace the authority of God in the life of the abused.
3. *The hypocrisy of not practicing what they teach.* The spiritual abuser will place demands upon the abused that they are not willing to practice themselves.

4. *Legalistic loads*. The demands of the spiritual abuser are heavy and burdensome. The focus is on obeying the legalistic rules of the spiritual abuser rather than grace-based obedience to God.

Grounding: 478 Breathing

Breathing exercises are a simple, effective way to regulate your nervous system. Breathing exercises abound, so there is no shortage of options. You can pick what works well for you. Cell phone apps can guide you through breathing exercises, so you might consider downloading one to expand your breathing repertoire.

One important tip is that you practice your breathing exercises regularly. Make it part of your routine, even when you feel good and think you do not need them. Remember, we need to practice these types of tools when we do not urgently need them so they are more readily available to us when we do.

478 Breathing

- Sit in a comfortable position, allowing your gaze to fall softly to the floor or close your eyes.
- Place a hand on your stomach.
- Take a slow breath through your nose, feeling the air in your nostrils as you inhale. Allow the breath to continue through your body into your stomach. Imagine you are blowing up an imaginary balloon in your stomach. Feel the hand resting on your stomach rise as the air fills the balloon. You can do this to a count of 4. You want your stomach to rise as you breathe.
    - Tip: If your shoulders or upper chest is rising, you are likely not taking a deep breath. Sometimes, it's easier to feel your stomach rising if you lie down.
- Once the balloon is full, hold your breath for a count of 7.

- Next, allow the air to gently escape through your mouth (as though you are gently blowing out a candle) until the balloon deflates as you count to 8.
- Feel free to allow a gentle hum or groan to release with the air.
- Repeat, building up to 5–10 minutes as you practice.
- Practice this skill daily. You can combine it with other grounding exercises.

Day 2: Your Story: The Web

Look back at day 1 and review the first two ways the spiritual abuser weaves a web of control. Answer the questions below about how the spiritually abusive relationship began.

A "Good" Beginning

Describe how you became involved in the spiritually abusive relationship or group.

Were there "good" experiences?

Initially, were any needs met? Perhaps you felt a sense of belonging, were searching for a place of spiritual growth, or enjoyed serving alongside others.

Did this initial "good" beginning make it difficult to leave? If so, explain why.

Self-Appointed "Divine" Authority

Spiritual abuse involves a misuse of power in a spiritual setting. A simple definition of power is "the capacity to influence."[1] Power can be used for good or for harm.

What are some areas in life where you have power?

In what areas of your life did the spiritual abuser have power?

Did the spiritual abuser claim to have final spiritual authority or "divine" authority in your life? If so, explain how.

---

[1] Peter Scazzero, *The Emotionally Healthy Leader* (Grand Rapids: Zondervan, 2015), 242.

What passages or theological teachings did the spiritual abuser employ to justify the claim for "divine" authority?

Can you think of a specific example? If so, please describe.

Day 3: Your Story: The Web

Turn to day 1 and review the third and fourth ways the spiritual abuser weaves a web of control.

The Hypocrisy of Not Practicing What They Teach

In Matthew 23:3, Jesus points out the behaviors and attitudes of a particular group of scribes and Pharisees: "Therefore do whatever they tell you, and observe it. But don't do what they do, because they don't practice what they teach." In this passage, the critique was not about the teachings. Instead, Jesus was critiquing their unwillingness to practice the teachings themselves.

Were there teachings or expectations placed on you that the spiritual abuser was unwilling to perform? If so, list those here.

Legalistic Loads

Spiritual abusers, much like the scribes and Pharisees in Jesus's day, place heavy, legalistic loads on their followers. Read the following passage from Matthew 23:

> They tie up heavy loads that are hard to carry and put them on people's shoulders, but they themselves aren't willing to lift a finger to move them. (v. 4)

List the "heavy loads" (rules and regulations) you were required to follow.

If you were to share an image of what the load felt like, what image would describe it? Feel free to draw the image.

Let's now contrast the heavy, burdensome load of the spiritual abuser to the yoke of Christ as you read the following passage:

> Come to me, all of you who are weary and burdened, and I will give you rest. Take my yoke upon you and learn from me, because I am lowly and humble in heart, and you will find rest for your souls. For my yoke is easy and my burden is light. (Matthew 11:28–30)

Perhaps you have seen a picture of a yoke. It can be worn by two animals, which places the burden on both carrying the load. Unlike the spiritual abusers who "aren't willing to lift a finger," Jesus is sharing the yoke. How does Jesus describe his yoke?

How does Jesus describe himself in this passage?

How does this contrast with the attitude of the spiritual abuser?

The recipients of this invitation are referred to as "weary and burdened." Through your spiritually abusive experience, you may have felt these two emotions deep in your soul. Jesus describes the impact of his yoke and learning from him as providing "rest for your souls." Take a minute to journal about the effects of spiritual abuse on your soul and how it might feel for your soul to have rest.

Day 4: Exploring Thoughts and Beliefs about God

We will explore your view of God and what beliefs about God may have developed as a result of the spiritually abusive experience.

Remember: If these activities become overwhelming, you are in charge and can put this workbook down at any time. Take a break as needed. Engage in your coping and grounding tools. You are doing difficult work.

The following beliefs may have developed:

- "I am unacceptable to God."
- "I am unlovable in God's eyes."

If you were to envision how God sees you right now, what would you imagine his posture and expression to be?

How has the spiritually abusive experience impacted the previous image?

I invite you to read the following passages:

> For you are saved by grace through faith, and this is not from yourselves; it is God's gift—not from works, so that no one can boast. For we are his workmanship, created in Christ Jesus for good works, which God prepared ahead of time for us to do. (Ephesians 2:8–10)

> For while we were still helpless, at the right time, Christ died for the ungodly. For rarely will someone die for a just person—though for a good person perhaps someone might even dare to die. But God proves his own love for us in that while we were still sinners, Christ died for us. (Romans 5:6–8)

What do the previous verses say about how we come to be accepted by God? About God's love for us?

Based on the above verses, how would you respond to a friend who confided in you that he or she does not feel acceptable or lovable to God?

Precious soul who is reading this workbook, I wish I could look into your eyes and tell you what I am about to write. God loves you. You do not have to earn his acceptance. He gives it freely and mercifully through Christ. You are invited to receive his love. He adores you. He created you in his image. You are priceless.

Day 5: Skills: Identifying Unhelpful Thinking Patterns

For our skill today, we will work on identifying unhelpful thinking patterns that can develop throughout life. In cognitive behavioral therapy, these are called "cognitive distortions."[2] I will share three this week, and we will review four additional patterns next week.

I provide a description and two examples of each type of thinking pattern. In the first example, I suggested a more effective or helpful way to think about the situation. Under the second example, you can rewrite the statement to a more effective way of thinking.

All-or-Nothing Thinking

- A situation is viewed as all good or all bad, completely acceptable or unacceptable.
- There is no continuum, so thoughts are polarized.
- Example: "I missed reading my Bible one day this week. I'm not a real Christian."

[2] Judith S. Beck and Aaron T. Beck, *Cognitive Behavior Therapy: Basics and Beyond*, 3rd ed. (New York: Guilford, 2020), 252–54.

    - More helpful thought: "I usually read my Bible daily, but it's okay to miss days sometimes."
- Example: "I did not make an A+ on the exam. I'm a failure."
    - More helpful statement: ______________________________

Catastrophic Thinking

- Predicting the worst-case scenario for a situation
- Example: "My stomach feels funny. I have a terminal illness."
    - More helpful thought: "Hmmm . . . I'm not feeling great. If it doesn't pass, I'll make a doctor's appointment to get it checked out."
- Example: "My daughter didn't answer my call. She has been in a terrible accident."
    - More helpful statement: ______________________________
- Do you have any catastrophic thoughts regarding faith or spirituality? If so, list below. Write the thought and the more helpful statement.

Should and Must

- You find yourself saying, I "should" do ________ or I "must" do ________, followed by an unrealistic expectation of yourself or critical thoughts about yourself.
- Example: "I should not be making mistakes."
    - More helpful statement: "Making mistakes is human. It's okay to make mistakes."
- Example: "To be a good Christian, I should [or must] pray for one hour."
    - More helpful statement: ______________________________

Which of these unhelpful thinking patterns may have formed or worsened during your spiritually abusive experience?

In the appendix at the back of the book is a thought log that combines what we have reviewed over the past few weeks. The directions for using it are included on the page following the log. Please turn to the page and look over it. Use it when you notice physical symptoms, difficult emotions, or unhelpful thoughts or thinking patterns.

Day 6: Holding Hope in Christ

The attitudes of spiritual abusers do not reflect the attitudes we need to have toward one another. They are drastically different. I invite you to read the following passage to explore the attitudes and actions God's Word instructs us to exhibit:

> Do nothing out of selfish ambition or conceit, but in humility consider others as more important than yourselves. Everyone should look not to his own interests, but rather to the interests of others. (Philippians 2:3–4)

What attitudes are we instructed to avoid?

What attitudes do we need to exhibit?

As you read the passages in this workbook, you may find some that were used against you. The previous passage may be one of those instances. If so, I invite you to journal about the experience.

Let's read about Christ, who demonstrated perfect humility and humble servanthood:

> Adopt the same attitude as that of Christ Jesus, who existing in the form of God, did not consider equality with God as something to be exploited. Instead he emptied himself by assuming the form of a servant, taking on the likeness of humanity. And when he had come as a man, he humbled himself by becoming obedient to the point of death—even to death on a cross. For this reason God highly exalted him and gave him the name that is above every name, so that at the name of Jesus every knee will bow—in heaven and on earth and under the earth—and every tongue will confess that Jesus Christ is Lord, to the glory of God the Father. (Philippians 2:5–11)

In your own words, contrast this description of Christ with the actions and attitudes of your spiritual abuser(s).

Day 7: Rest

Which pleasurable activity do you choose?

Week 4: Primary Takeaway

What is your primary takeaway from this week?

Week 5

CAUGHT IN A WEB (PART 2)

We will continue to explore how a spiritual abuser weaves a web of control that entraps the victim.

Our goals for the week:

- ❏ Focus of the week: Exploring the web of spiritual abuse
- ❏ Grounding: Using coping statements
- ❏ Your story: Exploring how you were caught in a web of spiritual abuse
- ❏ Exploring thoughts and beliefs about anger
- ❏ Skills: Unhelpful thinking patterns (part 2)
- ❏ Holding hope: God's intent for the shepherd and God as the Chief Shepherd
- ❏ Recommended reading from *Understanding Spiritual Abuse*: This week continues the information presented in chapter 3.

Day 1: Caught in a Web and Grounding

This week, we will explore four additional ways the spiritual abuser may entrap the victim in a web of control:

1. *Deceptive use of God's name and Scripture*
2. *Seeking self-promotion and praise.* Spiritual abusers are seeking positions of honor and authority. They seek self-exaltation rather than exalting Christ. Their ways rather than the ways of Christ. Pride over humility. Positions of honor over positions of service.
3. *Focus on outward appearance.* The focus of the spiritual abuser is more on outward appearances than matters of the heart and the spiritual condition of the victim.
4. *Instilling fear.* The spiritual abuser uses a variety of tactics to instill fear in the victim.

We will examine the first method today.

Deceptive Use of God's Name and Scripture

Spiritual abusers often deceptively misuse the name of God, Scripture, or theological teachings to gain control and justify their actions.

In what ways did the spiritual abuser misuse God's name, Scripture, or theological teachings to control? (For example, Scriptures such as Matthew 5:39; Matthew 18:21–22; and 1 Corinthians 6:1–2 may be used to demand a woman remain in an abusive marriage.)

Did the spiritual abuser misuse God's name, Scripture, or theological teachings to justify their actions? If so, please explain how.

Grounding by Using Coping Statements

What we say to ourselves matters. When you're feeling dysregulated, I invite you to speak to yourself the following phrases, or coping statements. I have provided several suggestions and a place for you to write your own. You will likely find a few that work best for you.

- This, too, shall pass.
- I can ride this wave until it passes.
- This feeling will not last forever.
- I can survive this.
- It's okay to feel _________.
- I can take some time to soothe myself.
- These feelings are painful, but they will eventually pass.
- I can use my coping tools.
- God is near to the broken hearted and saves those crushed in spirit (Psalm 34:18).
- I can pray that God will give me strength.
- God is my refuge and strength.
- I can pray for God's comfort.
- When I am weary, I can find rest in God.
- Perhaps there are additional phrases or Scripture passages that bring you comfort. Add them below.
- ____
- ____

Day 2: Your Story: The Web

Today, we will focus on a group of scribes and Pharisees who were seeking self-promotion and praise, in addition to their focus on outward appearance.

Seeking Self-Promotion and Praise

Continue reading in Matthew 23:

> They do everything to be seen by others: They enlarge their phylacteries and lengthen their tassels. They love the place of honor at banquets, the front seats in the synagogues, greetings in the marketplaces, and to be called "Rabbi" by people. (vv. 5–7)

In the previous passage, underline how these particular scribes and Pharisees seek self-promotion and praise.

The issue was not wearing phylacteries or tassels. Jewish males were instructed to do this to remind them of God's commands (Deuteronomy 11:18; 22:12; Numbers 15:38–39). The issue was that they were enlarging and lengthening them to appear more pious and gain honor and glory for themselves.

The issue was not attending banquets, going to the synagogue, or visiting the marketplace. The problem was that they sought titles of honor to increase their reputation and standing. They sought to bring glory and honor to themselves rather than God.

Read Jesus's instructions in Matthew 5:16:

> In the same way, let your light shine before others, so that they may see your good works and give glory to your Father in heaven.

According to this passage, what is the purpose of "letting our light shine" and of our "good works"? Notice the contrast of who is getting the glory.

In what ways did your spiritual abuser command the praise of others?

Focus on Outward Appearance

Continue reading Jesus's words in Matthew 23:

> Woe to you, scribes and Pharisees, hypocrites! You pay a tenth of mint, dill, and cumin, and yet you have neglected the more important matters of the law—justice, mercy, and faithfulness. These things should have been done without neglecting the others. Blind guides! You strain out a gnat, but gulp down a camel! (vv. 23–24)

The scribes and Pharisees addressed in this passage were neglecting some important matters. What "more important matters of the law" were neglected?

What important matters were neglected in your experience of spiritual abuse?

If applicable, describe how your spiritual abuser was straining gnats (following meticulous rules) while gulping down camels (ignoring more important matters).

Day 3: Your Story: The Web

Spiritual abusers instill fear to control their victims. We will identify the ways fear was instilled in your experience. In Matthew 23:33, Jesus refers to these scribes and Pharisees as "snakes" and a "brood of vipers."

When my daughter was in elementary school, we went on a field trip to a local nature area with boardwalks crossing the south Louisiana marshes. The swamps and marshes have a distinct beauty, particularly the moss-covered cypress trees, so I anticipated a lovely stroll with my daughter and her classmates. As we began walking, I noticed some creatures hanging in the trees, lying on the tree stumps, and lazing by the water. I could not believe my eyes. Snakes. Everywhere. There were actual piles of them, like big bowls of spaghetti, lying all over the place—mounds of spaghetti snakes. I was horrified. (Even more so by the alligators lounging alongside these clumps of snakes.) I know some people enjoy this, but I assure you that I did not. Even as I am typing this, I am shuddering at the thought of all those snakes (and gators!).

The thought of snakes instills fear in me, and the image of a brood of vipers reminds me of that horrifying day in the marsh. More shocking than my experience is the understanding of this term in its historical and cultural setting. Read the following excerpt from *Understanding Spiritual Abuse*:[1]

---

[1] Karen Roudkovski, *Understanding Spiritual Abuse: What It Is and How to Respond* (Brentwood, TN: B&H Academic, 2024), 82.

> Understanding the imagery from an ancient Mediterranean cultural perspective brings additional gravity. There was a widespread tradition that vipers killed their mother during birth ("parent-murder"), chewing their way out of her womb.[2] Keener states, "Ancient writers sometimes used parent-murder as an example of one of the worst conceivable crimes, one that invited divine vengeance."[3]

The attitudes and actions of these particular scribes and Pharisees can be compared to the current understanding of spiritual abusers. How does calling them a "brood of vipers" impact your understanding?

What fears did you experience during the spiritually abusive experience?

How did the spiritual abuser instill and maintain this fear?

Choose one grounding skill and complete it before you move on with your day. Our material today was heavy. Take care of yourself.

---

[2] See Craig S. Keener, "'Brood of Vipers' (Matthew 3.7; 12.34; 23.33)," *Journal for the Study of the New Testament* 28, no. 1 (2005), 7–8.

[3] Keener, 3.

Day 4: Exploring Thoughts and Beliefs about Anger

While working through this week's topic, you may have noticed some feelings of anger. Let's explore some general concepts about anger.

What were you taught about anger when you were a child?

What were you taught about anger in the spiritually abusive setting?

Anger can be referred to as a "secondary emotion." To illustrate this, think of an "anger iceberg." (If you type "anger iceberg" into an internet search engine, you will see numerous printable images of the anger iceberg.) Anger is like the part of the iceberg you see above the surface, but this is only the "tip of the iceberg." Underneath the surface are more vulnerable emotions you are also experiencing. We see the anger, but a lot more is happening inside. Some common emotions under the surface are fear, embarrassment, sadness, disappointment, helplessness, shame, loneliness, rejection, feeling unsafe, vulnerable, or hurt. Anger may also be an indication you are hungry or need sleep.

Anger can be motivating and may lead to healthy change or advocacy. The thoughts and emotions underlying anger may be the realization of injustice and a desire to seek justice, to speak up, and to advocate for yourself or others.

If you are feeling anger about your spiritually abusive experience, answer the following questions:

What are the emotions under the surface of the anger?

How is this anger impacting you and your relationships?

How is this anger motivating you? Are you motivated to set healthy boundaries? (We will explore this next week.) Are you inspired to raise awareness about spiritual abuse or advocate for survivors?

I encourage you to end today with one of your grounding tools.

Day 5: Skills: Unhelpful Thinking Patterns

Last week, we reviewed four unhelpful thinking patterns. Today, we will review an additional four.[4] I provided examples and invite you to add your own.

Mind Reading

- ➢ Imagining what another person is thinking
- ➢ Example: A colleague at work walks by your desk without smiling and saying hello. You think, "She thinks I didn't pull my weight on that last project. She is mad at me."
  - ❍ More helpful thought: "I can't read another person's mind. She didn't stop and say hello for many possible reasons."
- ➢ Example: "If I attend a new church and people find out I've not been to church in two years, they will think I'm not a Christian. They are going to think I don't fit in here."
  - ❍ More helpful thought: ______________________________

[4] See Judith S. Beck and Aaron T. Beck, *Cognitive Behavior Therapy: Basics and Beyond*, 3rd ed. (New York: Guilford, 2020), 252–54.

Personalization

- You blame yourself and take responsibility for other people's behavior or a situation you did not have control over.
- Example: Your teenager makes a poor decision, and you think, "It's all my fault. I'm a bad parent."
  - More helpful thought: "I am doing the best I can as a parent, but ultimately, my child will make his or her own choices."
- Example: "It's my fault that ________ happened."
  - More helpful thought: "What was actually in my control in that situation?"
- You may have the following beliefs about responsibility in your spiritually abusive experience:
  - "I am responsible (for what happened to me)."
  - "I should have known/done something."

  If you have these thoughts, what is a more accurate way to think about this? For example, "It is not my fault." "I am not responsible for the behaviors of the spiritual abuser."
- Can you think of another example from your own life?

Labeling

- Name-calling yourself or others
- Example: Someone you are meeting for lunch is twenty minutes late. You think, "She is rude and inconsiderate."
  - More helpful thought: "Maybe she got caught in traffic. I can ask her to call or text me if she is running late in the future."
- Can you think of another example from when you name-called yourself or someone else?

Overgeneralization

- Making a broad, sweeping statement

- Usually includes words such as: "always," "never," "all the time," "every," "forever," or "nothing." Pay attention to when you are using these words. Avoid making these types of generalizations.
- Example: You may see this as a criticism in marriage when someone says, "My wife never ______." Or "My husband always ______."
- Example: "Nothing ever goes my way."
- Can you think of other examples?

Which of these unhelpful thinking patterns may have formed or worsened during your spiritually abusive experience?

I encourage you to use the thought log in the appendix today. The directions are included on the page after the thought log. Continue using the thought log anytime you:

- Feel dysregulated
- Notice unhelpful thoughts or beliefs
- Notice unhelpful thinking patterns

If you consistently use the log, you will automatically begin to ask yourself the questions I included with the log. Over time, you will become more aware of your thoughts and emotions.

Day 6: Holding Hope in the Great Shepherd

In 1 Peter 5, we see Peter's appeal where the elders are instructed to "shepherd God's flock." Please read the following passage describing how they are to shepherd:

> I exhort the elders among you as a fellow elder and witness to the sufferings of Christ, as well as one who shares in the glory about to be revealed: Shepherd God's flock among you, not overseeing out of compulsion but willingly, as God would have you; not out of greed for money but eagerly; not lording it over those entrusted to you, but being examples to the flock. And when the chief Shepherd appears, you will receive the unfading crown of glory. In the same way, you who are younger, be subject to the elders. All of you clothe yourselves with humility toward one another, because
>
> > **God resists the proud**
> > **but gives grace to the humble.** (vv. 1–5)

I listed what they are instructed "not" to do on the left side of the chart below. Look at the Scripture above and fill in the chart with what Peter charges them to do instead.

What "not" to do	What to do instead
Do not oversee out of compulsion.	
Do not oversee out of greed for money.	
Do not lord over those entrusted to you.	

What is the instruction for everyone in verse 5?

Fill in the missing words: "God resists the ______ but gives grace to the ________________."

Let's conclude this week by reading about the Good, Merciful Chief Shepherd:

> The Lord is my shepherd;
> I have what I need.
> He lets me lie down in green pastures;
> he leads me beside quiet waters.
> He renews my life;
> he leads me along the right paths
> for his name's sake.
> Even when I go through the darkest valley,
> I fear no danger,
> for you are with me;
> your rod and your staff—they comfort me.
> You prepare a table before me
> in the presence of my enemies;
> you anoint my head with oil;
> my cup overflows.
> Only goodness and faithful love will pursue me
> all the days of my life,
> and I will dwell in the house of the Lord
> as long as I live. (Psalm 23:1–6)

Day 7: Rest

Which pleasurable activity do you choose?

Week 5: Primary Takeaway

What is your primary takeaway from this week?

Week 6

COERCIVE AND MANIPULATIVE CONTROL (PART 1)

Before beginning this week, read the definition of spiritual abuse I introduced in week 1.

Definition: Spiritual abuse is "a misuse of power in a spiritual context in which a person or group uses **various coercive and manipulative methods of controlling the victim,** resulting in the abused individual experiencing spiritual, emotional/psychological, physical, or relational harm."[1]

For the next two weeks, we will focus on the bolded part of the definition and the six areas of control exhibited by the spiritual abuser.

Our goals for the week:

- ❏ Focus of the week: Methods of coercive and manipulative control
- ❏ Grounding: Name 5

[1] Karen Roudkovski, *Understanding Spiritual Abuse: What It Is and How to Respond* (Brentwood, TN: B&H Academic, 2024), 15.

- ❑ Your story: Comparing the methods of control to what occurred in your situation
- ❑ Your story and tools: Exploring values
- ❑ Holding hope: A search for wisdom
- ❑ Recommended reading from *Understanding Spiritual Abuse*: Chapter 4 covers the topic of "control."

Day 1: Your Story: Control and Grounding

This week, we will review the first three methods of control. As we examine these areas and journal answers to questions about the methods of control, please keep in mind that not everyone experiences all of these methods of control, so you can skip over the questions that do not apply to your situation.

Following is a chart listing the methods of control on the left and the assessment statement that indicates this type of control. We will review one of these methods per day for the next three days.

Method of Control	Statement on the Spiritual Abuse Assessment
Control by limiting personal agency	I was NOT permitted to make my own decisions without approval.
Control by excessive accountability enforced by monitoring behavior	My behavior was constantly being monitored.
Control by performance-based acceptance	I had freedom to decline participation in an activity without fear of negative consequences.

Control by Limiting Personal Agency

When we have personal agency, we are responsible for our decisions and choices that are consistent with our values and beliefs. It is the "feeling of being in the driving seat when it comes to our actions."[2] If the spiritual abuser is highly controlling of decisions, then our sense of agency may be reduced. Our ability to make decisions can be impacted.

Did you have to seek permission for decisions? If so, list the decisions for which you had to seek permission.

After the spiritually abusive experience, what is the first decision you recall making on your own? What was that experience like for you?

Do you experience difficulty making decisions? If so, when did this difficulty begin or worsen?

Later this week, we will explore your personal values and apply them to decision-making next week.

---

[2] James W. Moore, "What Is the Sense of Agency and Why Does It Matter?," *Frontiers in Psychology* 7 (August 29, 2016): 1, https://doi.org/10.3389/fpsyg.2016.01272, as quoted in Roudkovski, *Understanding Spiritual Abuse*, 89.

Grounding: Name 5

For your grounding activity this week, we will review a grounding strategy similar to 54321. In this strategy, you name five things from a variety of categories. You can be creative and develop your categories or increase the number of items you name. Here are some examples:

- Name five sports teams.
- Name five types of birds.
- Name five movies.
- Name five types of flowers.
- Name five green vegetables.

Practice this skill with the examples above.

Day 2: Your Story: Methods of Control

Control by Excessive Accountability Enforced by Monitoring Behavior

Accountability can be helpful. Perhaps you ask a friend to hold you accountable for going to the gym four times per week. Or maybe you and your spouse are holding each other accountable to be in bed at a particular time so you are not exhausted the following day.

Accountability can extend to the spiritual. Perhaps you have a friend you check in with about how you are spiritually. Accountability is healthy and helpful when there are appropriate boundaries. But within a spiritually abusive setting, boundaries are violated. The accountability is excessive.

Let's explore your experience with accountability in the spiritually abusive experience:

In what areas were you held accountable?

At what point did you realize this was excessive?

How was your behavior monitored?

Who monitored your behavior?

Describe the thoughts and emotions you experienced while living in this situation of having your behavior monitored.

Are there areas of your life where you think healthy accountability would be helpful? Name those areas.

It is understandable if you are hesitant to engage in accountability. Journal about your concerns in the space below.

Day 3: Your Story: Methods of Control

Control by Performance-Based Acceptance

In a spiritually abusive relationship, your acceptance and approval are based on how you perform and participate according to the spiritual abuser's demands.

In what areas were you required to participate or "perform" to avoid negative consequences?

Did you want to participate in these activities? Or perhaps you initially wanted to participate, but something changed over time? Describe what this experience was like for you.

What was the consequence when you did not participate?

In the spiritually abusive situation, did you ever feel accepted without performance? If so, describe when this changed.

What negative consequences did you fear if you did not participate?

What negative consequences did you endure?

How has this impacted your willingness to volunteer your time?

What areas in your community or social circle might you find fulfillment and enjoyment in volunteering your time (e.g., watching a friend's child so she can have a free afternoon, volunteering at an after-school program, donating items or time to a shelter for victims of domestic violence)?

Day 4: Exploring Values

Being involved in a high-control situation may impact our ability to identify and live within our values and beliefs. I will allow you space today and tomorrow to brainstorm what is important in some general areas. Think about your values in specific terms. For example, if I value quality time with my friends, that value will require me to leave time in my schedule. Or, if I value honest and direct communication with my spouse, I can work on my personal communication skills to be a more effective communicator.

Relationships

Consider yourself in relationship with your family, friends, and community. Think about what matters to you in these relationships. For example, is it quality time spent together? Honesty? Traditions? Communication? Showing displays of love? How does your faith inform your values?

What is important to you in the following areas?
What are your values in your relationship with your spouse?

What are your parenting values?

Think of the other family relationships (e.g., parents, grandparents, siblings, nieces and nephews, grandchildren). What is important to you in those relationships?

What traits are essential to you in friendships?

What characteristics do you offer these relationships? Ask yourself, "What kind of friend, spouse, or parent do I want to be?"

How do you want to be involved with the community at large?

Faith, Spirituality, and Religious Involvement

Think about your beliefs and the expression of those beliefs.

What faith or spiritual practices do you find most meaningful? (We will explore these further in week 10.)

When in your life have you felt closest to God?

What practices were vital to you during that time?

What do you value in your religious involvement and faith community? (We will explore some safe and healthy community descriptors in week 12.)

Free Time and Fun, Hobbies and Interests

How do you want to spend your free time?

What hobbies do you currently enjoy or have you enjoyed in the past?

What activities do you find relaxing?

Are you spending the amount of time you would like on these activities?

Do you ever feel uneasy or guilty for simply relaxing? If so, be curious about that—where do you think that is coming from?

What interests would you like to explore? What are some actions you might take to begin this exploration?

Finances

Do you live within a budget where you decide how to spend your money?

Review your budget or spending and consider if it aligns with your values. For example, you may realize you do not use your cable subscription and would rather use the money to take a pottery class or learn to play an instrument.

Are you able to support causes that are important to you? What are those causes?

Day 5: Exploring Values

Today, let's continue our exploration of values.

Career, Education, and Training

- What is important to you in a career or job?

- Do you have any specific short-term or long-term career goals?

- Would you like to complete additional education or training? If so, what?

Personal Well-Being and Personal Growth

What do you value about your physical health (e.g., exercise, nutrition, sleep)?

What do you value about your emotional health?

What contributes to your overall well-being?

What areas of personal growth can you identify?

We have examined some broad categories of values. I invite you to look back and consider which values are nonnegotiable in their importance. Remember these when making decisions and setting goals for your life.

I hope these categories and questions advanced your exploration of personal values and beliefs. You can add your own as they come to mind. Spiritual abuse impacts a person's sense of agency, so be gentle with yourself as you explore areas of value and work through articulating what you believe.

Day 6: Holding Hope: Wisdom

When I think about values in life, I'm reminded of my need for wisdom. We will explore Scripture about wisdom both this week and next.

Wisdom is more than simply having knowledge; it is knowing how to apply that knowledge to a situation. How do you define wisdom?

Underline the phrases in the passages below that tell us how we gain wisdom:

For the LORD gives wisdom;
from his mouth come knowledge and understanding. (Proverbs 2:6)

The fear of the LORD is the beginning of wisdom,
and the knowledge of the Holy One is understanding. (Proverbs 9:10)

Arrogance leads to nothing but strife,
but wisdom is gained by those who take advice. (Proverbs 13:10)

> The one who walks with the wise will become wise,
> but a companion of fools will suffer harm. (Proverbs 13:20)

> Now if any of you lacks wisdom, he should ask God—who gives to all generously and ungrudgingly—and it will be given to him. (James 1:5)

Based on the passages above, how do we gain wisdom?

Read James 3:17 and underline how the wisdom of God is described:

> But the wisdom from above is first pure, then peace-loving, gentle, compliant, full of mercy and good fruits, unwavering, without pretense.

Notice how this description contrasts with the attitudes and actions exhibited by the spiritual abuser.

Read the following passage to explore the benefits of wisdom:

> Happy is a man who finds wisdom
> and who acquires understanding,
> for she is more profitable than silver,
> and her revenue is better than gold.
> She is more precious than jewels;
> nothing you desire can equal her.
> Long life is in her right hand;
> in her left, riches and honor.
> Her ways are pleasant,
> and all her paths, peaceful.
> She is a tree of life to those who embrace her,
> And those who hold on to her are happy. (Proverbs 3:13–18)

Eat honey, my son, for it is good,
and the honeycomb is sweet to your palate;
realize that wisdom is the same for you.
If you find it, you will have a future,
and your hope will never fade. (Proverbs 24:13–14)

In your own words, what are the benefits of wisdom?

Day 7: Rest

Which pleasurable activity do you choose?

Week 6: Primary Takeaway

What is your primary takeaway from this week?

Week 7

COERCIVE AND MANIPULATIVE CONTROL (PART 2)

You are at the halfway point of this study! Good work for your progress in this journey. As you move forward, continue caring for yourself by engaging your grounding skills or a pleasurable activity daily. This is hard work you are doing.

We continue our exploration of the methods of control used by the spiritual abuser. Our goals for the week are as follows:

- ❑ Focus of the week: We will review the remaining three methods of coercive and manipulative control.
- ❑ Grounding: Box breathing
- ❑ Your story: Exploring how the methods of control were used in your experience
- ❑ Exploring thoughts and beliefs about decision-making
- ❑ Tools: Value-informed decision-making

- ❑ Holding hope: We will continue our exploration of wisdom in the Bible.
- ❑ Recommended reading from *Understanding Spiritual Abuse*: This is a continuation of the material from chapter 4.

Day 1: Control and Grounding

Below is a chart listing the three additional methods of control on the left and the assessment statement that indicates this type of control on the right. We will review one of these methods per day for the next three days.

Method of Control	Statement on the Spiritual Abuse Assessment
Control by required obedience to the abuser	Obedience to the individual or group was required to avoid negative consequences.
Control by censuring	I was permitted to question the teachings of the individual or group without fear of retaliation.
Control by isolation	I was isolated from others outside the spiritual community or relationship.

Control by Required Obedience to the Abuser

The spiritual abuser demands obedience to himself or herself, justifying this required obedience through the use of Scripture or theological teaching. If the abused individual does not obey, negative consequences will follow.

In what areas of your life were you expected to obey the spiritual abuser?

Did you observe threats to the spiritual abuser's power and control? If so, how did that unfold?

If you challenged the spiritual abuser's power and control, what negative consequences did you face? I included a sample list below and left space for you to add your own.

- ❑ Public shaming
- ❑ Shunning
- ❑ Verbal attacks or threats
- ❑ Threats to your reputation
- ❑ Criticism of your spiritual walk (e.g., being told you were "backslidden")
- ❑ Gossip
- ❑ Name-calling (e.g., being called a "troublemaker" or "Jezebel")
- ❑ ______________________________
- ❑ ______________________________

What negative consequence(s) were the most difficult for you to experience?

How are the negative consequences impacting you in the present time?

Grounding: Box Breathing[1]

We will learn an additional breathing skill for grounding. This skill helps to calm your nervous system when dysregulated.

- ➢ Inhale to the count of 4. Allow the air to blow up an imaginary balloon in your stomach.
- ➢ Hold your breath for the count of 4.
- ➢ Exhale for the count of 4.
- ➢ Hold your breath after the exhale for a count of 4.
- ➢ Repeat for a few minutes until you begin to feel grounded.
- ➢ As you are counting and breathing, trace a square in the palm of your hand.
    - ❍ Inhale (for a count of 4) and trace one side of the square in the palm of your hand.
    - ❍ Hold (for a count of 4) while tracing another side of the square in the palm of your hand.
    - ❍ Exhale (for a count of 4) and trace the third side of the square.
    - ❍ Hold (for a count of 4) while tracing the final side of the square.
    - ❍ Repeat until you begin to feel grounded.

Day 2: Your Story: Methods of Control

Spiritual abusers silence the voices of victims. Let's examine how that occurred in your experience.

Control by Censuring

Questioning or raising concerns about the spiritual abuser's teachings, behaviors, or attitudes is met with some form of retaliation and negative consequences.

---

[1] See Mark Divine, *Unbeatable Mind: Forge Resiliency and Mental Toughness to Succeed at an Elite Level*, 3rd ed., upd. and rev. (Mark Divine, 2015), 45, 50–51.

Did you attempt to raise questions or concerns? If so, what questions did you raise?

How did the spiritual abuser respond to those perceived challenges?

What emotions are you experiencing as you describe the incident(s)?

How are those emotions being experienced in your body?

What are the accompanying thoughts about the spiritual abuser? About yourself?

What questions did you want to raise but did not because it felt unsafe? List those questions here.

Do you currently have any questions about faith or spirituality? If so, list them below. Consider where you might explore information regarding your questions from a trusted source.

Day 3: Your Story: Methods of Control

Control by Isolation

The spiritual abuser may isolate the victim from others outside the group. Or the spiritual abuser may isolate the victim from others within the group as a negative consequence for disobedience to the abuser or attempting to raise questions or concerns. The isolation may include limiting access to outside information. The isolation increases dependence on the abuser.

Did the spiritual abuser limit your access to information (e.g., media) outside the spiritually abusive setting?

How were you isolated from others outside the group?

Did this isolation impact your family relationships? If so, how?

Did this isolation impact your friendships? If so, how?

Were you isolated (or shunned) within a spiritually abusive group? If so, what was this experience like for you?

Were you told that you would be isolated from God? Or perhaps you felt isolated from God. Describe that experience.

If you were isolated, describe how you are working toward rebuilding a support system.

Day 4: Exploring Thoughts and Beliefs about Decision-Making

Individuals who experience the highly controlled nature of spiritual abuse may experience difficulty with decision-making. Consider whether or not there are certain areas where you struggle with making decisions. Are there particular areas where making decisions is more difficult?

You may have developed the following beliefs about your ability to make good decisions:

- I cannot trust myself to make good decisions.
- I cannot make good decisions.

A more helpful approach is the belief

- I can make informed decisions.

What are some decisions you are currently trying to make?

Are you experiencing difficulty making any of these decisions?

What are some additional thoughts or beliefs you have about decision-making?

Look over the list and place an asterisk on any time-sensitive decisions. You can also note the time frame for these decisions. Please choose one or two of these decisions to focus on tomorrow as we explore your decision-making process.

Day 5: Skills: Decision-Making

Based on your list from yesterday, what is a time-sensitive decision you are currently trying to make?

When making a decision, consider the following:

Name the decision you are trying to make.

What is the magnitude of this decision? For example, where to eat for dinner is a much lower magnitude than the decision to purchase a car.

What are your options or choices in this decision? List them.

Pray for wisdom, clarity, and peace.

What are the values that inform your decision? Rank them in order of importance.

Evaluate the choices based on your values. Ask yourself, "How do these choices align with my values?" Eliminate any options that are inconsistent with your values.

Make a "pro/con" or "risk/benefit" list for the remaining choices. Consider the cost. For example, what is the financial impact of the decision?

Evaluate the choices in light of your current circumstances and resources.

If this is a major decision, consider if you would benefit from consulting with someone you trust and respect who can provide an outside perspective but will not attempt to control your choice.

If you are feeling uneasy or confused, ask yourself, "Is this an urgent decision, or would it be best to allow myself some more time?"

Choose the best fit for your current situation. This decision may not always be the ideal solution. We are often doing the best we can with our resources.

Day 6: Holding Hope: Wisdom

Today, we continue our exploration of wisdom in Scripture, something we need when making decisions like those we reviewed yesterday.

Read the following passage:

> 19For the wisdom of this world is foolishness with God, since it is
> written, **He catches the wise in their craftiness**; 20and again, **The
> Lord knows that the reasonings of the wise are futile**. 21So let
> no one boast in human leaders, for everything is yours—22whether
> Paul or Apollos or Cephas or the world or life or death or things

> present or things to come—everything is yours, [23]and you belong to Christ, and Christ belongs to God. (1 Corinthians 3:19–23)

What warning about the "wisdom of the world" do we receive in this passage?

Reread verse 21. How does this apply to the spiritual abuser's attitude of seeking self-promotion and praise?

Read the following passage and underline the word that describes what accompanies wisdom:

> When arrogance comes, disgrace follows,
> but with humility comes wisdom. (Proverbs 11:2)

How is this different from the attitude of the spiritual abuser?

Read the following passage. Underline the words that describe wisdom that comes from "above."

> Who among you is wise and understanding? By his good conduct he should show that his works are done in the gentleness that comes from wisdom. But if you have bitter envy and selfish ambition in your heart, don't boast and deny the truth. Such wisdom does not come down from above but is earthly, unspiritual, demonic. For where there is envy and selfish ambition, there is disorder and every evil practice. But the wisdom from above is first pure, then peace-loving, gentle, compliant, full of mercy and good fruits, unwavering,

> without pretense. And the fruit of righteousness is sown in peace by those who cultivate peace. (James 3:13–18)

How is earthly wisdom described in the passage above?

In James 3:13–18, which terms best describe the "wisdom" of the spiritual abuser?

In what area(s) of your life do you need wisdom? How might you gain that wisdom?

Day 7: Rest

Which pleasurable activity do you choose today?

Week 7: Primary Takeaway

What is your primary takeaway from this week?

Week 8

IDENTIFYING HOLISTIC HARM

We now turn our attention to the impact of spiritual abuse and how it can cause holistic harm to the survivor. Read the definition of spiritual abuse.

Definition: Spiritual abuse is "a misuse of power in a spiritual context in which a person or group uses various coercive and manipulative methods of controlling the victim, **resulting in the abused individual experiencing spiritual, emotional/psychological, physical, or relational harm.**"[1]

Our goals for the week:

- ❑ Focus of the week: Exploring the holistic harm of spiritual abuse
- ❑ Grounding: Planting yourself in the present moment
- ❑ Your story: Naming the pain and harm
- ❑ Exploring thoughts and beliefs about suffering

---

[1] Karen Roudkovski, *Understanding Spiritual Abuse: What It Is and How to Respond* (Brentwood, TN: B&H Academic, 2024), 15.

- ❑ Tools: Lament
- ❑ Holding hope: Writing a prayer of lament
- ❑ Recommended reading from *Understanding Spiritual Abuse*: Chapter 5 explores the topic of "harm."

Day 1: Harm and Grounding

This week, we will focus on the statements on the Spiritual Abuse Assessment that reflect the harm caused by spiritual abuse. On days 2 and 3, we will explore the impact on your life.

Harm	**Statement on the Spiritual Abuse Assessment**
Overall sense of damage (This damage may be felt spiritually, emotionally/psychologically, physically, or relationally.)	I feel damaged by the experience.
Spiritual neglect	I believe my personal spiritual needs were neglected.
Physical symptoms	I experienced negative physical symptoms due to my negative spiritual experience.
Spiritual exploitation	My spiritual needs were exploited in order for the individual(s) to maintain power and/or control.
Blaming the victim	I was blamed for causing trouble when I questioned the actions or beliefs of the individual(s) in power.

I want to reemphasize the importance of caring for yourself while completing this workbook. As you explore the areas of harm, you may feel overwhelmed. You may also feel relieved to have the validation that your responses were to be expected and are commonly reported by others who have experienced spiritual abuse.

Take a few moments to journal about your thoughts and feelings as you read the above statements.

Grounding Tool: Planting Yourself in the Present Moment

- ➢ Sit upright in a chair.
- ➢ Roll your shoulder back into a relaxed position.
- ➢ Notice your face and jaw. Relax any tension.
- ➢ Firmly plant your feet on the floor. Wiggle your toes.
- ➢ Take a few deep belly breaths.
- ➢ As you exhale, notice the weight of your body firmly planted in your chair and your feet firmly planted on the ground in this present moment.
- ➢ Gaze around the room. What do you see? What do you hear? Use your senses.
- ➢ Pick up an object nearby (e.g., a pen, vase, coffee mug) and describe the object in detail. Notice how it feels in your hands. Describe the object's weight, color, texture, and temperature while you simultaneously notice your feet still firmly planted on the floor.

Day 2: Your Story: Naming the Pain and Harm

We are going to explore the ways that the spiritually abusive experience caused harm to you spiritually and the ways you were blamed for causing trouble if you raised concerns about the spiritual abuser's behavior.

The response to disclosures of abuse can cause further damage. Survivors have told me that the response to the disclosure of their abuse was as harmful (and, for some, even worse) as the spiritually abusive experience itself. That was my experience as well, and it was devastating.

We will also consider how you may have been spiritually neglected or spiritually exploited. Next week, you will have the opportunity to explore spiritual health.

Spiritual Harm, Spiritual Neglect, and Spiritual Exploitation

Check the following boxes that indicate ways you were impacted spiritually. The list is not exhaustive. If you experienced a spiritual impact I did not list, you can write it in the blank space provided.

- ❏ The spiritual abuser attempted to take the place of God in my life.
- ❏ Scripture or theological teachings were used against me.
- ❏ The spiritual abuser justified his or her actions using Scripture or theological teachings.
- ❏ The spiritual abuse has negatively impacted my image of God.
- ❏ I have difficulty accepting that God loves me.
- ❏ I feel betrayed by God.
- ❏ I feel abandoned by God.
- ❏ I constantly fear being punished by God.
- ❏ I struggle with knowing what I believe about God and faith.
- ❏ I have difficulty engaging in a religious community, such as a Bible study or church.
- ❏ My spiritual needs were ignored and neglected.
- ❏ My desire for spiritual growth and community was exploited to meet the needs of the spiritual abuser.
- ❏ I was accused of being "backslidden" when I questioned what was happening.
- ❏ I feared being publicly discredited or humiliated.

- ❑ I was publicly discredited or humiliated.
- ❑ The spiritual abuser (or others) gossiped about me.
- ❑ I have a deep sense of shame.
- ❑ My emotional/psychological (or physical) symptoms of the spiritual abuse were considered sinful.
- ❑ Certain religious objects, symbols, or activities are emotionally dysregulating, or I would consider them to be trauma triggers (e.g., certain Scriptures, religious songs, church services, or symbols of faith).
- ❑ I have difficulty envisioning healthy spirituality.
- ❑ ______________________________
- ❑ ______________________________

Reviewing the items you marked above, what have been the most challenging impacts?

Name specific ways this is impacting you now. (The impact may be spiritual, emotional/psychological, physical, or relational.)

Describe what healing in these areas would look like.

Blame

Another aspect of harm is being blamed for causing trouble if you question what is happening. Check off the ways you experienced blame. Write any additional ways in the blank space provided.

- ❑ When I reported a problem, I became the problem.
- ❑ The spiritual abuser claimed he or she was the victim. "You are not the victim; I am the victim. You are attacking me."
- ❑ The spiritual abuser had a "defense team" that defended him or her.
- ❑ I was accused of doing something to cause the abuse.
- ❑ I was told I was not being "submissive" enough to authority.
- ❑ I was accused of being a troublemaker.
- ❑ I was told that I would destroy the spiritual abuser's ministry or reputation.
- ❑ I was accused of destroying the "unity" of the church or organization.
- ❑ I was told I would destroy the ministry of the church or organization.
- ❑ ______________________________
- ❑ ______________________________

Reviewing the items you marked above, what have been the most challenging impacts?

Name specific ways this is impacting you now. (The impact may be spiritual, emotional/psychological, physical, or relational.)

Describe what healing in these areas would look like.

Day 3: Your Story: Naming the Pain and Harm

Today, we are going to continue exploring the harm caused by spiritual abuse. We will focus on the relational, emotional/psychological, and physical areas of harm.

Relational Harm

Spiritual abuse impacts your relationships, both inside and outside of the spiritually abusive situation. Check off the ways you have experienced the impact. Write any additional ways in the blank space provided.

- ❑ I was isolated from others outside of the spiritually abusive relationship.
- ❑ I was shunned within my church (or other group) for questioning the spiritual abuse.
- ❑ I feel isolated.
- ❑ I am lonely.
- ❑ I feel betrayed.
- ❑ I have difficulty trusting others.
- ❑ I feel disconnected.
- ❑ I lost my community.
- ❑ My relationships outside the spiritually abusive situation suffered or were neglected because of the demands of the spiritual abuser.
- ❑ I am experiencing difficulty reengaging in relationships.
- ❑ My marriage relationship was negatively impacted.
- ❑ My parenting was negatively impacted.
- ❑ I feel guilt or regret for exposing my children to a spiritually abusive setting.
- ❑ I regret following the parenting advice of the spiritual abuser.

- ❑ I grew up in a spiritually abusive situation.
- ❑ ______________________________
- ❑ ______________________________

Reviewing the items you marked above, what have been the most challenging impacts?

Name specific ways this is impacting you now. (The impact may be spiritual, emotional/psychological, physical, or relational.)

Describe what healing in these areas would look like.

Emotional/Psychological Harm

Spiritual abuse impacts our emotional/psychological well-being. If applicable, check off the ways you experienced emotional/psychological harm. Write any additional ways in the blank space provided.

- ❑ Fear
- ❑ Shame
- ❑ Anxiety
- ❑ Regret
- ❑ Sadness
- ❑ Grief
- ❑ Guilt
- ❑ Confusion
- ❑ Anger

- ❑ Depression
- ❑ Irritability
- ❑ Hypervigilance
- ❑ Difficulty concentrating
- ❑ Intrusive, unwanted memories about the spiritually abusive situation
- ❑ ______________________________
- ❑ ______________________________

Reviewing the items you marked above, what have been the most challenging impacts?

Name specific ways this is impacting you now. (The impact may be spiritual, emotional/psychological, physical, or relational.)

Describe what healing in these areas would look like.

Physical Symptoms

Finally, we can experience physical symptoms of the spiritually abusive situation. When we experience trauma, we can have physical symptoms. When we are suffering emotionally or relationally, our body complains. Check off the ways you experienced physical symptoms. Write any additional symptoms in the blank space provided.

- ❑ I have difficulty falling asleep.
- ❑ I wake up during the night and cannot fall asleep.
- ❑ I have nightmares.
- ❑ I am having stomach issues.
- ❑ I am experiencing headaches.
- ❑ I feel "on edge."
- ❑ I have tightness in my chest or throat when I think about the experience.
- ❑ I have experienced panic attacks.
- ❑ I feel tired, lethargic, or unmotivated.
- ❑ ______________________________
- ❑ ______________________________

Reviewing the items you marked above, what have been the most challenging impacts?

Name specific ways this is impacting you now. (The impact may be spiritual, emotional/psychological, physical, or relational.)

All of these symptoms can be indicative of health issues. If you have not had a physical checkup with your doctor, today would be an excellent time to schedule an appointment to take care of yourself physically.

Day 4: Exploring Thoughts and Beliefs about Suffering

Today, we are exploring the concept of suffering. How would you define "suffering"?

Suffering may present itself in a variety of ways. Abuse. Oppression. Mental or physical illness. Grief. Loss. No person is immune from suffering. Those who experience spiritual abuse have suffered deeply.

What do you consider to be the most challenging time(s) of suffering in your life?

What was the most challenging aspect of those times?

What were you taught about suffering?

What are your current beliefs about the purpose of suffering?

Everyone suffers at some point in life. When suffering, it can be difficult to process what we are going through and to have language for our pain, particularly if we are in a setting that views suffering as weakness.

Several years ago, I experienced an issue that required emergency surgery on both of my eyes. During the several months between multiple surgeries, I was instructed to only lie in certain positions. As you might imagine, I did not rest well. I had difficulty falling asleep and would often wake up during the night. When I woke up in the dark room, I would have a moment of panic, thinking I had completely lost my vision. The most helpful action that calmed me, particularly at first, was to listen to the Bible while falling asleep and when I woke up at night. Occasionally, I would listen to sermons or Christian podcasts. When I think back to those nights, I remember the sadness and fear, but I also have a deep sense of peace and appreciation for feeling the presence and comfort of God during those dark nights.

Despite multitudes of prayers and skilled surgeons, one of my eyes could not be restored, leaving me with some long-term challenges. As I came to terms with my new sight, I visited a church where my husband was preaching. Numerous kind individuals told me how they had been praying for my sight. What an encouragement! However, one individual approached me with an admonishment that my eyes would be healed once I listened to God and what he was trying to teach me. The comment hurt. Little did that person know I had been spending incredibly deep times with God. I do not know what this person's theology of suffering entails, but this comment revealed some information about that person's view of suffering.

Is suffering a sign of weakness? Does it mean I will no longer suffer once I get everything "right"? Many people live with suffering for countless reasons: health conditions, grief and loss, lack of safe living conditions, and much more. Suffering is part of life in a fallen world. Those who live will suffer. Paul suffered. Christ suffered. God can be glorified through our suffering.

James 1:2–4 is one of the passages I am most encouraged by:

> Consider it a great joy, my brothers and sisters, whenever you experience various trials, because you know that the testing of your faith produces endurance. And let endurance have its full effect, so that you may be mature and complete, lacking nothing.

What does this Scripture say is the product of trials that we experience? Let's read one more:

> Therefore, since we have been justified by faith, we have peace with God through our Lord Jesus Christ. We have also obtained access through him by faith into this grace in which we stand, and we boast in the hope of the glory of God. And not only that, but we also boast in our afflictions, because we know that affliction produces endurance, endurance produces proven character, and proven character produces hope. This hope will not disappoint us, because God's love has been poured out in our hearts through the Holy Spirit who was given to us. (Romans 5:1–5)

What does this passage say is produced in our afflictions?

At times, in suffering, we do not feel closer to God. Instead, we might feel alone and forgotten. Tomorrow, we will examine how to take our suffering and pain before God, even when we feel utterly abandoned.

Day 5: Skills: Lament

I write this section with the understanding that this activity is challenging. We are going to approach God with our pain. If you raised questions or concerns to your spiritual abuser and received retaliation for doing so, bringing your pain before God may feel uncertain and unsafe.

We will use a process we see in Scripture to bring your pain, suffering, and complaints (yes, complaints!) before God. This process is called "lament." I consider lamenting one of our most incredible opportunities to come before God when we are desperately hurting and grieving.

Over one-third of the book of Psalms is made up of psalms of lament, providing an example of sharing our pain, questions, and complaints with God. Lament consists of five basic steps.[2] In the Psalms, you will find that the steps are not always in this order, nor does a psalm of lament always contain each component. But here is a general structure that we will use:

1. *Address.* At the onset, it is vital to address Yahweh, the one true God.
2. *Complaint.* In complaint, you are invited to share your emotions and thoughts with God.
3. *Confession of trust.* In this stage, you express your trust in God. After a spiritually abusive experience, trust can be shattered. Because a spiritual abuser attempts to take the place of God in your life, your image of God is impacted. So, this step may be exceptionally difficult for a survivor of spiritual abuse.
4. *Petition.* Make your request to God.
5. *Vow of praise.* Express your commitment to praise God.

Let's explore an example of lament from Scripture: Psalm 55. This psalm may be entitled "Betrayal by a Friend." In the psalm, David expresses his deep pain over the betrayal of a trusted friend.

Spiritual abuse is a betrayal trauma because the abuser is someone who is trusted and has spiritual power and authority. Betrayal trauma typically has more damaging consequences than abuse perpetrated by a stranger because of the betrayal by a person or institution that you trusted. As you

---

[2] Stephen C. Torr, "A Winnicottian Approach to Biblical Lament: Developing a True Self in the Midst of Suffering," *Journal of Psychology and Theology* 47, no. 1 (March 2019): 48–65, https://doi.org/10.1177/0091647118795184.

read, notice the strong imagery and look for the five components of lament listed above.

> God, listen to my prayer
> and do not hide from my plea for help.
> Pay attention to me and answer me.
> I am restless and in turmoil with my complaint,
> because of the enemy's words,
> because of the pressure of the wicked.
> For they bring down disaster on me
> and harass me in anger.
> My heart shudders within me;
> terrors of death sweep over me.
> Fear and trembling grip me;
> horror has overwhelmed me.
> I said, "If only I had wings like a dove!
> I would fly away and find rest.
> How far away I would flee;
> I would stay in the wilderness.
> I would hurry to my shelter
> from the raging wind and the storm."
> Lord, confuse and confound their speech,
> for I see violence and strife in the city;
> day and night they make the rounds on its walls.
> Crime and trouble are within it;
> destruction is inside it;
> oppression and deceit never leave its marketplace.
> Now it is not an enemy who insults me—
> otherwise I could bear it;
> it is not a foe who rises up against me—
> otherwise I could hide from him.
> But it is you, a man who is my peer,
> my companion and good friend!

We used to have close fellowship;
we walked with the crowd into the house of God.
Let death take them by surprise;
let them go down to Sheol alive,
because evil is in their homes and within them.
But I call to God, and the LORD will save me.
I complain and groan morning, noon, and night,
and he hears my voice.
Though many are against me,
he will redeem me from my battle unharmed.
God, the one enthroned from long ago,
will hear and will humiliate them
because they do not change
and do not fear God.
My friend acts violently
Against those at peace with him;
he violates his covenant.
His buttery words are smooth,
but war is in his heart.
His words are softer than oil,
but they are drawn swords.
Cast your burden on the LORD,
and he will sustain you;
he will never allow the righteous to be shaken.
God, you will bring them down
to the Pit of destruction;
men of bloodshed and treachery
will not live out half their days.
But I will trust in you. (Psalm 55:1–23)

How does the psalmist address God?

What are his complaints?

What petitions (requests) does he make?

What confessions of trust and vows of praise does he make?

Circle all the expressions of emotion in the psalm.

List the images used to describe God.

List the images used to describe the betrayer.

Underline images that describe the suffering.

Which image can you most relate to in your own experience?

Tomorrow, you will write out your own prayer of lament.

Day 6: Holding Hope: Writing a Prayer of Lament

Today, I invite you to write a prayer of lament about the harm caused by your spiritually abusive experience. I provide the components below, but you do not need to follow this structure in the order provided.

1. Address (God):

2. Complaint: Share your emotions and thoughts with God. Share what you are actually thinking and feeling, not what you think you "should" be thinking and feeling. Express the grief over your experiences. Share your losses (e.g., friendships, trust, safety).

3. Confession of trust: Write an expression of trust in God. For example, see Psalm 55:16 from yesterday's reading. "But I call to God, and the LORD will save me." If you are struggling with trusting God, write about your struggle.

4. Make a petition or request of God: What are you asking of God in this situation? Do you desire healing? Understanding? Justice? Ask this of God.

5. Praise: Express your commitment to praise God. If you are struggling in this area, write about how this is difficult.

Week 8: Primary Takeaway

What is your primary takeaway from this week?

Day 7: Rest

Which pleasurable activity do you choose?

Week 9

YOUR SPIRITUAL TIMELINE

Throughout this workbook, you have been journaling about the impact of spiritual abuse on your life. This week, you will construct a spiritual timeline.

Our goals for the week:

- ❏ Focus of the week: Your spiritual history
- ❏ Grounding: The present-moment walk
- ❏ Your story: Constructing your spiritual timeline
- ❏ Exploring thoughts and beliefs about your value and worth
- ❏ Skills: Journaling
- ❏ Holding hope in God's enduring presence
- ❏ Recommended reading from *Understanding Spiritual Abuse*: No reading this week.

Day 1: Spiritual Timeline and Grounding

Our focus this week is on your spiritual history. We will explore your spiritual history through the development of a spiritual timeline. Timelines help us work through difficult experiences, such as spiritual abuse. By constructing a timeline, you can see how the experience fits into the "big picture" of your life and allows you to think about what experiences were most formative and impactful on your life today.

You may discover that not all events on your timeline are negative. There will be some positive events in addition to the difficult ones. You'll recall that even within a spiritually abusive situation, there can be positive aspects, particularly at the beginning. The early positive experiences are one reason why it is so easy to become entrapped in a spiritually abusive experience.

For some of you, this timeline will include your involvement with a formal religious group or parachurch organization, such as a mission agency or Christian school. For others, the focus of the timeline will be on spiritual abuse within a marriage or family. Others may focus on spiritual abuse in a discipleship or mentorship relationship. For some, the spiritual abuse may have occurred while you were a minister. Regardless of where the spiritual abuse occurred, I want you to begin your spiritual timeline from childhood. We will start this timeline tomorrow.

Grounding: The Present-Moment Walk

This week's grounding will take longer than usual, but this is one of my favorite grounding activities. I want you to go outside. Hopefully, today is a nice day. If it is raining, you may need to sit on a covered patio or porch to complete the activity. The goal is to walk outside while focusing on the present moment. If you have a small yard, you can use the space you have. Perhaps you could repeat this activity at a local park or nature center one day. A present-moment walk is a beautiful way to calm your nervous system and release some tension in your body. With your senses, observe the following:

- What do you see?
- What do you hear?
- What smells do you notice?
- What is the temperature like on your skin?
- What do you notice in your body as you are walking?
- What thoughts come to your mind?
- What emotions are you experiencing?
- Are you experiencing any distractions or difficulties while doing this activity? If so, what are they, and how are you responding?

Day 2: Your Story: Your Spiritual Timeline

We will spend today and tomorrow constructing your timeline.

Your spiritual timeline may intersect with the experience of other abuse and trauma. It is your choice to add the other traumatic events that occurred. My greatest concern is that you remain safe while completing any part of this workbook. If this activity becomes too painful or dysregulating, you can stop anytime. You might find that working with a therapist would be a helpful addition at this point in your journey.

Some individuals are detailed in their timelines, while others list only the basics. This is your timeline. There is no right or wrong answer, so include events that are significant to you and place them according to how you perceived the event at the time it occurred.

Directions

- Draw a line through the middle of a blank piece of paper.
- Begin at your earliest memories.

- In chronological order, write significant positive spiritual experiences above the line.
- Write negative experiences below the line.
- You can include items such as the following:
  - Your first memory of church
  - Any additional memories of church that stand out in your mind
  - What was your first introduction to God? How old were you? Who first taught you about God?
  - Who taught you about God throughout your childhood? Add those individuals to your timeline.
  - Salvation/conversion experience
  - Baptism
  - Religious camps
  - Religious holidays
  - Include any memorable or formative religious or spiritual events in your life.
  - What was your first introduction to the spiritual abuser or spiritually abusive community? Does the experience begin "good"?
  - When was the first time you remember thinking, *Whoa! This isn't right*, or sensed a "red flag"? Add that moment to your timeline.
  - Add any additional significant events that occurred during your spiritually abusive experience (e.g., a formal meeting, an informal exchange, events you were required to attend).
  - If you expressed concern, add this to the timeline. You can add multiple times of concern if desired.
  - When did you first realize you needed to remove yourself from the situation?
  - When did you leave the spiritually abusive situation (if this applies to you)?

- ❍ Continue filling in the timeline with significant spiritual events since your departure. For example, did you begin attending church again? Continue this until you reach the current time.

Constructing a timeline can be dysregulating, so choose one grounding activity or one pleasurable activity to do now. Maintain awareness of how you feel (emotionally and physically) for the rest of the day. This is hard work, so treat yourself kindly.

Day 3: Your Story: Your Spiritual Timeline

Today, we will look at your timeline as a whole.

What are the three most challenging times? Describe them below.

What are three positive experiences? Describe them below.

What three events do you consider the most impactful? These events may be the same as your challenging or positive experiences. For example, a person may consider their conversion experience one of the three positive experiences in addition to one of the three most impactful.

Looking back to the challenging experiences, describe what helped you through those times. What brought you comfort and hope?

How do the events of your timeline (both positive and challenging) inform your view of God?

What are three lessons you have learned about spirituality (or religion) throughout your life?

Day 4: Exploring Thoughts and Beliefs about Your Value and Worth

Our spiritually abusive experiences impact our thoughts and beliefs about our value and worth. Spiritually abusive relationships are performance-based. To some extent, you might notice that society at large can be heavily performance-based, so you may see the interwoven impact from multiple origins. Even in parenting, commending a child solely on their performance is common.

In a performance-driven setting, we may hold beliefs such as these:

- "My value is based on my performance."
- "I need to earn love/acceptance."

- "I will never be good enough."
- "I am damaged."
- "I am a failure."
- "I am unlovable in God's eyes, and in others'."
- "God or others will reject me."
- "I am unworthy of love."

Do you have any additional thoughts or beliefs related to your value and worth?

If you have any of these underlying beliefs, you may find yourself

- people pleasing
- basing your well-being on how others perceive or accept you
- being afraid to say no
- feeling as though you need to earn someone's love or acceptance
- believing your need to earn love and acceptance extends to God himself
- feeling shame

When we feel shame, we often go into hiding. We isolate ourselves from others. We avoid vulnerability. The connections we need as humans—the connections we were created to experience—are severed. The spiritual abuser often uses the powerful tool of shame to control and isolate the victim.

Have you experienced feelings of shame? Describe the impact.

In what ways has being in a performance-based setting impacted you?

When these thoughts and beliefs come up, you can use the following method:

- Notice
- Be curious ("Hmmm . . . Is that what I really believe to be true?")
- Ask yourself, "Who told me that?"
- Replace it with a truthful statement.

This exercise may be challenging at first. Remember, you are forging new paths in your brain.

Let's brainstorm some truthful statements you can remind yourself of when you notice the untruthful beliefs about value and worth are impacting you. I will get you started, and you can add more as you think of them.

- "God created me with worth and value."
- "I am valuable just as I am."
- "I do not need to earn God's love."
- "I do not need to earn the love of others."
- ____

In preparation for tomorrow's activity, choose one of the beliefs listed above that you struggle with believing.

Day 5: Skills: Journaling

Yesterday, you chose one belief about your value and worth that you struggle with believing. Today, consider the following question and journal your response in the space provided below:

- How would my life be different if I saw myself as described in this statement?

As you think about that question, consider the following: How would your decision-making be different? Your relationships? How you view yourself? How you view yourself in relation to others? How you view yourself in relation to God?

Journal entry:

Day 6: Holding Hope: God's Enduring Presence

As you review your timeline, there may have been times when you felt alone. I invite you to read the passage below about the enduring presence of God.

Underline the words and phrases that describe God in this passage. Take some time to journal in the space below.

> Jacob, why do you say,
> and Israel, why do you assert,
> "My way is hidden from the Lord,
> and my claim is ignored by my God"?
> Do you not know?
> Have you not heard?
> The Lord is the everlasting God,
> the Creator of the whole earth.
> He never becomes faint or weary;
> there is no limit to his understanding.
> He gives strength to the faint
> and strengthens the powerless.
> Youths may become faint and weary,
> and young men stumble and fall,
> but those who trust in the Lord
> will renew their strength;
> they will soar on wings like eagles;
> they will run and not become weary,
> they will walk and not faint. (Isaiah 40:27–31)

What strength are you needing right now? Take some time to journal.

Day 7: Rest

Which pleasurable activity do you choose today?

Week 9: Primary Takeaway

What is your primary takeaway from this week?

Week 10

UNDERSTANDING SPIRITUAL HEALTH

What is spiritual health? That question is our focus of the week. We cannot fully cover the topic in this space, but I will introduce it. Our goals for the week:

- ❑ Focus of the week: Spiritual health
- ❑ Grounding: Leaves on a stream
- ❑ Your story: Exploring healthy spirituality and setting goals
- ❑ Exploring thoughts and beliefs about emotional and spiritual health
- ❑ Skills: Circles of control
- ❑ Holding hope: Cast your cares
- ❑ Recommended reading from *Understanding Spiritual Abuse*: No reading this week

Day 1: Spiritual Health and Grounding

Spiritual abuse can negatively impact our spiritual well-being. In healing, I invite you to consider how you define spiritual health. There are many components that you might consider as you build your understanding.

Check off the following spiritual disciplines and practices you consider essential to your spiritual health. I left some blanks for you to add additional ideas.

- ❏ Prayer
- ❏ Reading and studying Scripture
- ❏ Memorizing Scripture
- ❏ Practicing sabbath (a day of rest)
- ❏ Fasting
- ❏ Meditation
- ❏ Corporate worship
- ❏ Individual worship
- ❏ Participating in a faith community (e.g., small group Bible study, church, prayer group, service group)
- ❏ Service to others
- ❏ ______________________________
- ❏ ______________________________

In addition to the spiritual disciplines and practices listed above, consider the ideas listed below that are a part of overall well-being. Notice we are moving into other areas of life (e.g., physical, relational, emotional). Because we are holistic beings, the areas listed below can impact your spiritual health and vice versa.

- ❏ Taking time for pleasurable activities and hobbies
- ❏ Journaling
- ❏ Living according to your values and beliefs

- ❑ Friendships with others who strengthen or encourage your faith
- ❑ Showing empathy to others
- ❑ Ability to identify emotions
- ❑ Healthy communication and interpersonal tools
- ❑ Taking care of your physical body:
    - ❍ Sleep
    - ❍ Exercise
    - ❍ Nutrition
    - ❍ Medical care
- ❑ Setting healthy boundaries
- ❑ ____________________
- ❑ ____________________

Choose one or two items from the list above. How does that area impact your spiritual well-being?

In your own words, what does it mean to be spiritually healthy?

Grounding

For today's grounding tool, we will practice an exercise called "leaves on a stream."[1]

- ➢ Close your eyes and imagine yourself sitting by a gentle, flowing stream.

[1] See Russ Harris, *ACT Made Simple: An Easy-to-Read Primer on Acceptance and Commitment Therapy*, 2nd ed. (Oakland, CA: New Harbinger, 2019), chap. 15.

- Take some deep, slow breaths.
- Look around and notice what you see.
- Listen to the water lapping against the rocks.
- Now imagine leaves floating in the water, slowly drifting downstream.
- As thoughts enter your mind, place each thought on a leaf and observe how it drifts further from your sight.

You can use this tool whenever you are experiencing unwanted and unhelpful thoughts.

Day 2: Your Story: Exploring Healthy Spirituality

Last week, you developed your spiritual timeline. Looking back at the timeline, was there a time when you considered yourself spiritually healthy? If so, describe that time in the space below.

In the present, what spiritual disciplines would enhance your spiritual health?

How can you engage in these spiritual disciplines while avoiding legalism or performance-based acceptance?

What areas would enhance your overall well-being, which also impacts your spiritual health?

Choose one area you want to begin working on this week from the list provided on day 1. Tomorrow, we will set a SMART goal related to this area.

Day 3: Your Story: Setting Goals

Did you choose an area that you want to incorporate into your life? Perhaps it is meditation, prayer, or Scripture reading. Or, maybe you want to get better sleep or provide your body with better nutrition. For others, you may aim to improve your communication tools with others or set healthy boundaries. Choose one, and let's focus on it today. We are going to set a SMART goal related to your choice.[2]

SMART goals are

- ➢ Specific: Be specific in naming the goal.
- ➢ Measurable: The progress can be measured.
- ➢ Attainable: The goal should be achievable for you.
- ➢ Relevant: The goal relates to your life and what is important to you right now.
- ➢ Time-bound: A clearly defined timeline exists for measuring and achieving the goal.

Example: Let's imagine that I wanted to begin a regular practice of Scripture reading. I included an example of a SMART goal below.

- ➢ Specific: Scripture reading: I want to read the Gospel of John in one month.

---

[2] See G. T. Doran, "There's a S.M.A.R.T. Way to Write Management's Goals and Objectives," *Management Review* 70, no. 11 (1981): 35-36.

- Measurable: I will read one chapter per day.
- Attainable: Reading the Gospel of John in one month is attainable. With only twenty-one chapters, I can even miss a few days and still accomplish my goal.
    - Example of a goal that would not be attainable: I may set a goal to run a marathon four weeks from now. The goal is specific, and I can measure progress along the way and at the end. But, for me, this goal is not attainable. I would need more time to prepare for such a long race, mainly since I'm not a runner.
- Relevant: The goal is relevant because I want to prioritize my spiritual life.
- Time-bound: I set the manageable goal to finish the book in one month.

Now it's your turn!
Choose one goal and complete the following:

- Specific: ______________________________
- Measurable: ______________________________
- Attainable: ______________________________
- Relevant: ______________________________
- Time-bound: ______________________________

Day 4: Exploring Thoughts and Beliefs about Emotional and Spiritual Health

In week 2, we covered the topic of emotions. At times, people attempt to separate their emotions from their spirituality.

Take a few moments to think back on what you believe about the connection between our emotions and our spiritual health.

Do you have any unhelpful beliefs in this area? Some examples might include the following:

- Some emotions are "good," and others are "bad."
- If I am spiritually mature, I will never experience difficult or "bad" emotions.
- My emotions have nothing to do with my spiritual life.
- ____________________

Peter Scazzero writes about how God may speak to us through our physical responses to emotion: "God speaks to us through a knot in the stomach, muscle tension, trembling and shaking, the release of adrenaline into our bloodstream, headaches, and a suddenly elevated heart rate. God may be screaming at us through our physical body while we look for (and prefer) a more 'spiritual' signal."[3]

Describe the relationship between emotions and healthy spirituality.

[3] Peter Scazzero, *Emotionally Healthy Spirituality: It's Impossible to Be Spiritually Mature, While Remaining Emotionally Immature*, updated ed. (Grand Rapids: Zondervan, 2017), 71.

Review the unhelpful thoughts above. Replace the three examples above with truthful and helpful statements.

- ➢ ______________________________
- ➢ ______________________________
- ➢ ______________________________

Day 5: Skills: Circles of Control

Today, we will do an activity called "circles of control."[4] This exercise will help you evaluate what is actually in your control in certain circumstances. Realizing what is in your control is an aspect of emotional, spiritual, and relational health.

- ➢ Think of a situation that is concerning you right now.
- ➢ In the center circle, write down the things about that situation that are in your control. We can only control our own behaviors, thoughts, attitudes, decisions, and words.
- ➢ In the outer circle, write down the things about the situation that are out of your control. The behaviors, thoughts, attitudes, decisions, and words of others are out of our control. There may be areas where you have influence. But ultimately, you are not in control of others.
- ➢ Focus your time and energy on the areas in your control.
- ➢ If you are currently worried about an issue, I encourage you to complete this activity to develop a plan of action based on the things within your control.

[4] See Stephen R. Covey, *The 7 Habits of Highly Effective People*, 30th anniv. ed. (New York: Simon & Schuster, 2020), 89–103.

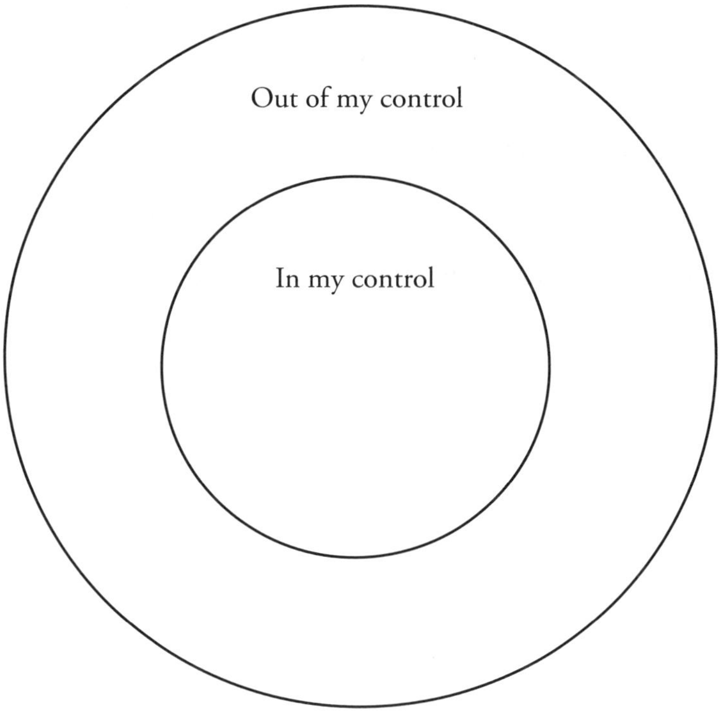

Day 6: Holding Hope: Cast Your Cares

In week 5, we examined 1 Peter 5:1–5, addressed to the elders who were to "shepherd." Today, we will explore verses 6–11.

> Humble yourselves, therefore, under the mighty hand of God, so that he may exalt you at the proper time, casting all your cares on him, because he cares about you. Be sober-minded, be alert. Your adversary the devil is prowling around like a roaring lion, looking for anyone he can devour. Resist him, firm in the faith, knowing that the same kind of sufferings are being experienced by your

> fellow believers throughout the world. The God of all grace, who called you to his eternal glory in Christ, will himself restore, establish, strengthen, and support you after you have suffered a little while. To him be dominion forever. Amen.

What does the passage tell us to do with our cares (v. 7)?

Imagine casting your cares toward God. Identify your cares. What are you casting?

Notice that verse 7 says "all." Do you want to cast any more cares you did not list above?

After we cast our cares toward God, what are we instructed to do next (vv. 8–9)? Why?

In verse 10, we see that Christ will restore, establish, strengthen, and support.

What areas of your faith and life do you need to be restored, established, strengthened, and supported?

Day 7: Rest

Which pleasurable activity do you choose?

Recommended Reading

Scazzero, Peter. *Emotionally Healthy Spirituality: It's Impossible to Be Spiritually Mature, While Remaining Emotionally Immature*. Grand Rapids: Zondervan, 2017.

Week 10: Primary Takeaway

What is your primary takeaway from this week?

Week 11

WHEN FORGIVENESS IS WEAPONIZED

Forgiveness is a complex topic to consider. My reason for including the issue of forgiveness in this workbook is that spiritual-abuse survivors have often had this topic weaponized against them. Your spiritual abuser or other individuals may have used Scriptures about forgiveness against you in an attempt to defend or excuse the behavior of the spiritual abuser. As a result, this topic may be particularly painful.

I want to give you space to think about your beliefs about forgiveness. Feel free to read over this material, consider it, and return to it again later. Like many topics in this workbook, I am introducing the concept, but processing it takes time.

Our goals for the week:

- ❑ Focus of the week: Forgiveness
- ❑ Grounding: Music
- ❑ Your story: Exploring forgiveness
- ❑ Exploring thoughts and beliefs about forgiveness

- ❑ Skills: Identifying and journaling about ways you were hurt
- ❑ Holding hope: The forgiveness of God
- ❑ Recommended reading from *Understanding Spiritual Abuse*: No reading this week

Day 1: What Is Forgiveness?

Individuals who have experienced spiritual abuse often report having Scripture and teachings on forgiveness used against them. Instead of responding well to their concerns or disclosures of spiritual abuse, forgiveness is weaponized against them as a way to prevent the spiritual abuser from facing the consequences of their behavior.

The purpose of this week is to provide you space to begin your thought process about forgiveness and define what you believe about forgiveness.

Defining Forgiveness

As you consider the act of forgiveness, let's explore what forgiveness is *not*:

- ❑ Forgiveness does not minimize the pain. Instead, it acknowledges the depths of the pain.
- ❑ Forgiveness does not mean you will never experience pain over the situation in the future.
- ❑ Forgiveness does not mean you will forget what happened.
- ❑ Forgiveness does not mean you will not realize additional hurts in the future.
- ❑ Forgiveness is not restoration of the relationship, nor does it mean you will reestablish the relationship in any way.

Consider Four Aspects of Forgiveness

- ❑ **Recognize** the pain and hurt. Forgiveness is costly. Name the offenses and how they were harmful. Acknowledge the cost.
- ❑ **Relinquish** the right to retaliate. Definitions of forgiveness often contain some form of this concept. In forgiveness, we relinquish our right to get even, but this does not mean justice should not be served or abuse should not be reported. All abuse, including spiritual abuse, needs to be reported. At times, the actions against us are illegal. In those cases, the justice system should be engaged to ensure the individual receives consequences and others are protected from further harm. This concept of forgiveness may be misused by the spiritual abuser and their defense team as a way of protecting the spiritual abuser. When this happens, the harm to the victim is compounded.
- ❑ **Release** our anger and resentment toward the person. Feelings of anger and resentment when we are wronged are normal and expected. Recognizing and processing those emotions is important. But dwelling on them long-term can be detrimental to our well-being.
- ❑ **Renew** our commitment. Forgiveness is a process, so each time we are reminded of the wrongs, we can renew our commitment to forgive based on our reasons for offering forgiveness.

How would you define forgiveness?

Grounding: Music

This week, I invite you to build a song playlist of encouraging or soothing music.

Day 2: Your Story: Exploring Forgiveness

It is difficult to forgive someone who asks for forgiveness. But forgiveness can be even more complex and challenging when someone does not recognize they have wronged you. In my work with spiritual-abuse survivors, I have observed that spiritual abusers often do not recognize the harm they cause. Or, they may give the survivor a disingenuous false apology to silence the individual.

Was the practice of forgiveness used against you, or did you receive a false apology from the abuser to silence you? Journal about the experience below.

Throughout this book, we have considered the spiritual, emotional/psychological, relational, and physical harm caused by spiritual abuse. Now, I invite you to consider how you might want forgiveness to look in the case of your spiritual abuse. Are you holding on to unspoken or unprocessed anger and resentment in a way that further harms you? If so, how is it impacting you in the following areas?

How is holding on to anger and resentment impacting you spiritually?

What is the emotional/psychological impact?

Relationally, is it impacting any other relationships?

What is the physical impact?

Your overall well-being can be negatively impacted by holding on to anger and resentment. If applicable, describe a time in your life when holding on to resentment affected you negatively. Is this currently happening?

Some individuals who experience spiritual abuse may blame themselves. They may ask, "Why did I get involved with that person (or group) in the first place?" or, "Why didn't I leave sooner?" If you raised your children in a spiritually abusive setting, you may experience deep regret, remorse, and anger not only toward the person or group but toward yourself as well.

Are you experiencing any anger and resentment turned inward? If so, describe this experience in the space below and what it might look like to release that anger toward yourself.

Day 3: Your Story: Exploring Forgiveness

In week 5, we explored the topic of anger and the concept that anger can be a motivating emotion. On the other hand, holding on to anger and resentment long-term can be detrimental to your well-being. Try journaling about any anger or resentment you are holding. Consider how this anger might be used as a motivator but not held on to long-term. If you are not currently experiencing anger, then journal about any potential triggers for anger in the future. Write your thoughts and feelings in the space below.

When you finish journaling, complete a grounding activity (see list in the back of the book) before continuing your day. Write what you chose in the space below.

Day 4: Exploring Thoughts and Beliefs about Forgiveness

In a spiritually abusive relationship, scriptures are often misused to control. Scriptures about forgiveness may be misused to silence a victim who is trying to advocate for himself or herself or others.

Were Scriptures about forgiveness used against you? Passages such as the ones below are used to prevent victims of spiritual abuse from speaking out about the abusive situation, to silence them. Or they may be used to threaten eternal consequences. The spiritual abuser, or his or her defense team, may say, "You need to forgive and let this go . . . if you want God to forgive you." Or, "You are causing trouble. Scripture says to live peaceably with everyone." Read the passages below:

> For if you forgive others their offenses, your heavenly Father will forgive you as well. But if you don't forgive others, your Father will not forgive your offenses. (Matthew 6:14–15)

> Do not repay anyone evil for evil. Give careful thought to do what is honorable in everyone's eyes. If possible, as far as it depends on you, live at peace with everyone. Friends, do not avenge yourselves; instead, leave room for God's wrath, because it is written, **Vengeance belongs to me; I will repay**, says the Lord. But
>
> > **If your enemy is hungry, feed him.**
> > **If he is thirsty, give him something to drink.**
> > **For in so doing**
> > **you will be heaping fiery coals on his head.**
>
> Do not be conquered by evil, but conquer evil with good. (Romans 12:17–21)

What do you believe is the meaning of these passages? You might find it helpful to use a commentary or study Bible to help you reflect on the meaning of these passages so as to better see how they were misused by the spiritual abuser.

In general, what were you taught about forgiveness in the spiritually abusive relationship?

How does that teaching differ from the definition you wrote about forgiveness on day 1?

Were any additional passages about forgiveness used against you? Please describe.

Describe a time when you forgave someone. What was that process like for you?

Day 5: Skills: Recognizing the Hurt and Grief

A significant aspect of forgiveness often overlooked is naming and recognizing the hurt and grief.

In the space below, journal about the damage caused by the spiritual abuser. Include the following information:

- Name the hurt(s) and losses. Give specific examples.
- Name the way each hurt or loss impacted you at the time.
- Name the way each hurt or loss impacts you in the present.

Journal using the prompts above.

Day 6: Holding Hope: The Forgiveness of God

Let's read a few passages about the merciful forgiveness of God. As you read, underline the words and phrases that describe God's forgiveness.

> Compassion and forgiveness belong to the Lord our God, though we have rebelled against him and have not obeyed the LORD our

God by following his instructions that he set before us through his servants the prophets. (Daniel 9:9–10)

Who is a God like you,
Forgiving iniquity and passing over rebellion
for the remnant of his inheritance?
He does not hold on to his anger forever
because he delights in faithful love. He will again have compassion on us;
he will vanquish our iniquities.
You will cast all our sins
into the depths of the sea. (Micah 7:18–19)

The LORD is compassionate and gracious,
slow to anger and abounding in faithful love.
He will not always accuse us
or be angry forever.
He has not dealt with us as our sins deserve
or repaid us according to our iniquities.
For as high as the heavens are above the earth,
so great is his faithful love
toward those who fear him.
As far as the east is from the west,
so far has he removed
our transgressions from us.
As a father has compassion on his children,
so the LORD has compassion on those who fear him. (Psalm 103:8–13)

If we confess our sins, he is faithful and righteous to forgive us our sins and to cleanse us from all unrighteousness. (1 John 1:9)

Based on these passages, describe God's forgiveness of us.

In what ways do these verses influence your view of forgiveness?

As we conclude our overview of forgiveness this week, take a few minutes to consider the following: Is forgiveness of your spiritual abuser something you want to consider? And, if you forgive your spiritual abuser, what are your reasons for doing so? Scripture? Benefit to your well-being? Wanting to move past the situation? Shifting your focus away from the person who wronged you? A combination of reasons? Write about your reasons in the space below.

What is the most challenging part of forgiveness for you?

Day 7: Rest

Which pleasurable activity do you choose?

Week 11: Primary Takeaway

What is your primary takeaway from this week?

Week 12

CHARACTERISTICS OF A SAFE COMMUNITY

Welcome to the final week of our journey through this workbook! This week, we will focus on safe and healthy spiritual communities through the following goals:

- ❑ Focus of the week: A review of eleven descriptors of spiritually abusive communities contrasted with the antidote for each
- ❑ Grounding: Reviewing your favorite coping strategies
- ❑ Your story: Exploring safe and healthy community
- ❑ Exploring your thoughts and beliefs about theological teachings
- ❑ Skills: Writing a letter to your former and future self
- ❑ Holding hope: God's design for healthy community
- ❑ Recommended reading from *Understanding Spiritual Abuse*: In chapter 11, I address the topic of "safe community."

Day 1: A Safe and Healthy Community

In the following chart, you will see the description of a spiritually abusive relationship on the left and a description of the healthy community on the right. This week, we will explore each of these and how you might envision yourself surviving and flourishing within a community that exhibits these characteristics. No community will perfectly show these characteristics, but you are looking for patterns.

Spiritual Abuse: Abuse of Power to Control	**Healthy Behaviors: Servant Leadership**
Control by limiting personal agency	Personal agency encouraged
Control by excessive accountability enforced by monitoring behavior	Healthy accountability for everyone
Control by performance-based acceptance	Grace- and love-based acceptance
Control by required obedience to the abuser	Obedience to God
Control by censuring	Questions encouraged and engaged
Control by isolation	Relational health encouraged
Harm—an overall sense of damage	Emotional health encouraged
Harm—spiritual neglect	Spiritual health encouraged
Harm—physical symptoms	Acceptance of limits and boundaries
Harm—spiritual exploitation	Honest and direct communication
Harm—blaming the victim	Acceptance of personal responsibility

We will begin exploring the "rules" of healthy versus unhealthy communities. For the remainder of this week, we will examine the eleven areas of a healthy faith community, as seen in the chart above.

All systems and relationships have "rules," including communities of faith. Some rules are spoken, while others are unspoken. Some rules are healthy, while others are unhealthy.

Here are three rules you might find in an unhealthy system.[1] I left space for you to add additional rules you may have observed in your experience.

- Keep the peace at all costs.
- Do not cause trouble.
- Protect the system (organization, church) at the expense of individual members.
- ____
- ____

Healthy systems have rules like the following: (I left space for you to add your own.)

- Questions are welcome, even if they are difficult.
- Bringing attention to abusive behaviors is encouraged.
- People are prioritized over maintaining the system.
- ____
- ____

Grounding

Throughout this workbook, you have learned grounding tools and developed a list of pleasurable activities. You have used the emotion chart, emotional temperature, and a thought log. You developed a repertoire of healthy coping tools. Name three to five coping tools you have found most helpful.

---

[1] Karen Roudkovski, *Understanding Spiritual Abuse: What It Is and How to Respond* (Brentwood, TN: B&H Academic, 2024), 183–84.

1. ______________________________
2. ______________________________
3. ______________________________
4. ______________________________
5. ______________________________

Today, I want to recommend an additional coping strategy. I have provided journal prompts on specific topics at various points in this workbook. I recommend purchasing a journal that you can use as needed to process your thoughts and feelings as you continue your healing journey.

Day 2: Your Story: Exploring Healthy Community

Personal Agency Encouraged

In week 6, we explored the concept of personal agency. In a healthy spiritual community, people are encouraged to study Scripture, ask questions, and make decisions consistent with their beliefs and convictions.

As you finish this workbook, describe any additional insight you have gained about personal agency within a spiritual community. What would be different than when you were in the spiritually abusive situation?

Healthy Accountability for Everyone

Leaders are not exempt from healthy accountability. Describe your view of what healthy accountability might look like in a spiritual community.

List some areas in which you believe healthy accountability is essential.

Grace- and Love-Based Acceptance

Performance is not a requirement for acceptance. Members willingly serve one another and their community based on their love for others.

Describe a time when you felt accepted, valued, and loved by a person or group.

Obedience to God (Rather than Obedience to the Spiritual Abuser)

How would you describe to someone what obedience to God looks like?

Questions Encouraged and Engaged

People are not shamed or shunned for asking questions. There are no negative consequences for raising concerns. Questions and concerns are engaged in a non-defensive manner.

What type of questions do you believe are essential to have the freedom to ask (without negative repercussions) in a healthy community?

Day 3: Your Story: Exploring Healthy Community (Continued)

Relational Health Encouraged

Healthy communities encourage healthy relationships both inside and outside the community. Consideration is given to the time you need to spend in these other relationships, with the understanding that it may prevent you from having unlimited availability.

What are some relationships you value right now?

How do you want to grow in these relationships?

Emotional Health Encouraged

How can emotional health be encouraged and supported in a spiritual community?

Spiritual Health Encouraged

Describe what spiritual health within a spiritual community would look like for you.

Acceptance of Limits and Boundaries

Boundaries are components of overall health: emotional, relational, spiritual, and physical.

What are your time limits in a spiritual community?

What are your privacy boundaries in a spiritual community?

Describe any other limits or boundaries that are important to you.

Honest and Direct Communication

Communication is direct, honest, and non-manipulative. If you raise a concern or question, describe what a response with healthy communication would look like.

Acceptance of Personal Responsibility

Everyone takes responsibility for their own actions and asks for forgiveness when needed. Have you ever received a genuine, sincere apology? What was that experience like for you?

Write about what it would look like if you were in a community like I described. What would be the first sign that you have entered a healthy spiritual community?

Day 4: Exploring Thoughts and Beliefs about Theological Teaching

When you enter a new community, you also engage in a system of theological beliefs. A system of beliefs is a way the group builds cohesiveness and an agreed-upon mission or purpose. A marker of a healthy community is that their beliefs are clearly explained and readily available to anyone. Additionally, leadership is available to discuss or clarify any beliefs you would like to explore more deeply.

If you are attending a church, find the statement of faith and read it. Or, if you are considering a church, find their statement of faith. This statement may be titled differently for various churches and denominations, so you may see it listed under a different title. The denomination may also have a statement of faith, so I encourage you to look for that document. You can contact the pastor for a copy if you cannot locate it on the website. You can even request an appointment with the pastor to discuss the document. In some churches, these are reviewed during new-member training before joining the church, which is a healthy practice.

As you review the documents, look for the beliefs about topics such as God, Scripture, salvation, and mission. Begin to read and study these areas for yourself as you regain your sense of agency and enjoy the freedom to explore and ask questions. Find resources written by experts in the field. Study and learn.

Day 5: Skills: Writing a Letter to Your Former Self and Future Self

Today I invite you to write two letters. This activity may take some time, so feel free to take a few days to complete it, but I encourage you to prioritize writing these.

To your former self: First, write a letter to your former self while you were going through the spiritually abusive experience. Express to yourself the empathy you needed to hear. Tell your younger self words of encouragement that are meaningful to you. Remind yourself that while this will forever change you, that healing is possible. Maybe include some things you have learned on your journey through this workbook. Be kind to yourself as you write.

To your future self: Second, write a letter to yourself for days in the future when you feel discouraged and the pain is triggered. Add some words of encouragement or insights that have been helpful. Add any Scripture that was helpful or encouraging. Think of this letter as how you might encourage a friend who is having a tough day in their journey of spiritual-abuse recovery. Keep this letter available to read when you have one of those days.

Day 6: Holding Hope: Healthy Community

We will end our final week reading representative passages describing healthy faith communities. I encourage you to search your Bible for more. As you read, underline the attitudes and actions described in the three passages below.

The words of Jesus:

I give you a new command: Love one another. Just as I have loved you, you are also to love one another. By this everyone will know that you are my disciples, if you love one another. (John 13:34–35)

A description of the early believers:

They devoted themselves to the apostles' teaching, to the fellowship, to the breaking of bread, and to prayer. Everyone was filled with awe, and many wonders and signs were being performed through the apostles. Now all the believers were together and held all things in common. They sold their possessions and property and distributed the proceeds to all, as any had need. Every day they devoted themselves to meeting together in the temple, and broke bread from house to house. They ate their food with joyful and sincere hearts, praising God and enjoying the favor of all the people. Every day the Lord added to their number those who were being saved. (Acts 2:42–47)

Instructions for our attitudes and actions:

Therefore, as God's chosen ones, holy and dearly loved, put on compassion, kindness, humility, gentleness, and patience, bearing with one another and forgiving one another if anyone has a grievance

> against another. Just as the Lord has forgiven you, so you are also to forgive. Above all, put on love, which is the perfect bond of unity. And let the peace of Christ, to which you were also called in one body, rule your hearts. And be thankful. Let the word of Christ dwell richly among you, in all wisdom teaching and admonishing one another through psalms, hymns, and spiritual songs, singing to God with gratitude in your hearts. And whatever you do, in word or in deed, do everything in the name of the Lord Jesus, giving thanks to God the Father through him. (Colossians 3:12–17)

In your own words, write a simple description of what you desire to find in a healthy faith community.

Each week, I invited you to write your primary takeaway from the week. In the spaces below, write three to five takeaways from the workbook from the past twelve weeks. Feel free to add more than five.

1. ______________________________
2. ______________________________
3. ______________________________
4. ______________________________
5. ______________________________

Week 12: Primary Takeaway

What is your primary takeaway from this week?

Day 7: Rest

Which pleasurable activity do you choose?

FINAL THOUGHTS

Survivors, I am grieved over the pain you have endured under the auspice of faith, religion, and spirituality, not to mention the misuse of the name of God himself. While writing the book and workbook, my keyboard has felt many teardrops. The heaviness has been palpable.

I also have hope for myself and for you.

I pray you will continue to heal.
I pray you will find peace in God's merciful, loving presence.
I pray for healthy spiritual relationships and safe faith communities.

Thank you for entrusting me with a portion of your journey.

APPENDIX

Pleasurable Activities

1. Walk or stand barefoot in the grass. Notice what you see, smell, hear, and feel.
2. Pray or write out a prayer.
3. Heat a shoulder wrap and place it on your shoulders. Add a drop or two of your favorite essential oil scent.
4. Ground with 54321.
5. Browse through a bookstore or library.
6. Have lunch outside (with no technology).
7. Meet a friend for coffee.
8. Call a friend.
9. Lift weights.
10. Jog or walk.
11. Ride a bike.
12. Go swimming.
13. Learn a new sport.
14. Move your body through an enjoyable physical activity.
15. Plant or care for a garden (vegetables or flowers).
16. Read your favorite Scripture.
17. Spend some time journaling.
18. Relax yourself with a deep breathing exercise (478, box, and any others you learn).
19. Spend a few moments in meditation.
20. Have a mug of tea while gazing out the window, noticing nature.

21. Get a massage.
22. Visit a museum.
23. Spend time with your pet.
24. Draw or doodle.
25. Enjoy a fine art coloring book.
26. Cook a favorite meal.
27. Try a new recipe.
28. Work a puzzle.
29. Listen to a podcast.
30. Make a playlist.
31. Listen to music.
32. Practice your peaceful place imagery.
33. Play an instrument.
34. Sing a favorite song.
35. Learn how to play a new instrument.
36. Write a song or poem.
37. Hug someone you love.
38. Go to counseling.
39. Take a nap.
40. Watch funny videos.
41. Play a board game.
42. Take photographs.
43. Knit or crochet.
44. Take a bath or shower.
45. Read a book.
46. Write a note of encouragement to yourself.
47. Write a note of encouragement to someone else.
48. Keep a gratitude journal.
49. Write a letter to someone who made a positive difference in your life. (Sending it is optional.)
50. Find a prayer, saying, or quote that is encouraging to you. Begin a place in your journal where you can add these quotes to read as needed.

51. Do a chore you have been putting off.
52. Organize a drawer or area of your house.
53. Gather some items for donation.
54. Go to a local park for a walk or picnic.
55. Get cozy. Wear comfortable clothes, turn on soothing music or a relaxing show, and eat a nourishing, comforting meal (i.e., chicken noodle soup, a fruit/bread/cheese board).

Emotions

Happy	Sad	Angry	Shame	Peaceful	Afraid	Loved	Rejected	Awe
Playful	Miserable	Annoyed	Embarrassed	Calm	Shock	Connected	Abandoned	Wonder
Joyful	Sorrowful	Irritated	Humiliated	Relaxed	Unease	Secure	Lonely	Humble
Creative	Grief	Jealous	Disgraced	Content	Terrified	Accepted	Excluded	Reverent
Ecstatic	Miserable	Enraged	Self-conscious	Serene	Anxious	Recognized	Disregarded	Surprise
Delight	Anguish	Furious	Mortified	Quiet	Petrified	Known	Unwanted	Amazed
Pleasure	Gloomy	Livid	Regret	Still	Dread	Seen	Discarded	Astonished
Carefree	Bothered	Fuming	Guilt	Tranquil	Distress	Valued	Forsaken	Admiration
Curious	Empty	Offended	Disappointed	Comfortable	Panic	Respected	Neglected	Veneration
Satisfied	Tired	Frustrated	Foolish	Cozy	Concern	Appreciated	Deserted	Worshipful
Amused	Discouraged	Distraught	Uncomfortable	Grounded	Apprehension	Esteemed	Snubbed	Respectful
Glad	Unfulfilled	Outraged	Remorse	Grateful	Nervous	Cherished	Ignored	Relief
Energetic	Depressed	Upset	Demeaned	Fulfilled	Powerless	Treasured	Forgotten	Release
Courageous	Bored	Bitter	Disgust	Inspired	Vulnerable	Trusting	Hurt	Empowered
Refreshed	Sorrow	Skeptical	Degraded	Humble	Fragile	Believed	Wounded	Inspired

Thought Log

Event	Emotion(s)	Temp? 0–100	Grounding?	Thought(s)	How True? 0–100%	Unhelpful Thinking Pattern(s)	Alternative thought?	How True? 0–100%	Emotion(s)	Temp? 0–100

Thought Log Guide

- ➢ Name the triggering event.
- ➢ Name the emotion(s).
- ➢ What is your emotional temperature? (0–100 percent)
- ➢ Do you need a grounding activity? If so, list the one(s) you use.
- ➢ Name your thought(s)
- ➢ On a scale of 0 to 100 percent, with 0 being not true at all and 100 being completely true, how true do you believe this thought to be?
- ➢ Name any unhelpful thinking patterns.
- ➢ What is an alternative way of thinking about this situation? What is a more helpful thought?
- ➢ How true do you believe the helpful thought to be now? (0–100 percent)
- ➢ What are your emotions now?
- ➢ What is your emotional temperature? (0–100 percent)
- ➢ What action do you want or need to take (if any)?

Group Leader's Guide

Group Guidelines

Having a set of guidelines and expectations is essential. Below is a list of some general group guidelines. Discuss these with your group and decide if there is anything else you would like to add. Following these suggestions will help keep the group helpful and safe and allow time for everyone to interact.

In the introductory session, take the time to review each guideline. Ask each member to check each box below as you review the guidelines. The checkmark is their agreement to follow the guidelines.

- ❑ Speak from an "I" position.
- ❑ Be aware that each person will have a unique spiritual and faith journey. It is important to set aside judgment about how participants are processing.
- ❑ Allow time for each person to share.
- ❑ Do not interrupt someone's sharing time or try to "fix" the person as he or she is sharing.
- ❑ This group is meant for active participation, not passive observance. If you are not comfortable sharing with the group, it is okay to share your concerns and start slow. It is normal to have difficulty trusting others after spiritual abuse. Your group can take small steps toward building trust.

- ❑ What is shared in the group stays in the group. Absolutely no gossiping and sharing with others outside the group.
- ❑ The exception to confidentiality is if you express an intent to harm yourself or others. Additionally, all mandatory reporting laws will be followed.
- ❑ Make every effort to show up on time for your group session so that individuals who may be vulnerably sharing are not interrupted.
- ❑ Turn off or silence your cell phones. (Understandably, those on call for work, who have children in childcare, or who have other special circumstances will need to remain accessible.)
- ❑ Are there any additional guidelines your group would like to set?

Online Group Guidelines

There are additional things to consider if you choose to meet online. Follow the general guidelines listed above and the following online group etiquette.

- ➢ Consider the privacy of others. Attend the group in a private location where no one else can hear what is said.
- ➢ Wear headphones.
- ➢ Do not use public Wi-Fi.
- ➢ Keep your camera on.
- ➢ Turn off your microphone if you are not speaking.
- ➢ Avoid doing other activities while in the group (e.g., washing dishes, folding laundry). Keep your focus on the group.
- ➢ Are there any additional guidelines your group would like to set?

Recommended Size and Time Commitment

Group Size: I recommend you cap the group at eight participants, plus two group leaders. This size will allow enough time for everyone to participate but still allow enough members to continue for the week if there are absences. Two leaders are helpful in case someone becomes emotionally dysregulated and needs to step outside. One leader can leave with the individual and offer assistance to that participant.

Time Commitment: This group will meet for thirteen weeks. The first week is an introductory week. The recommended meeting time is ninety minutes.

Note: If you are doing this group during an hour-long discipleship or Bible study meeting at your church, request members make arrangements to come early or stay late. You may need to work with the church's childcare workers to allow additional time.

One issue to be aware of for those who have experienced a high-control, spiritually abusive organization or relationship is that your comfort level in a group may be impacted. For example, spiritual abusers typically dole out consequences for asking questions. In that case, it may be uncomfortable for you to share your thoughts and opinions about the material or when group members begin sharing diverse points of view.

A Note to Group Leaders: Before beginning this group, have a referral list of professional counselors in your area to recommend to group members needing additional support.

Group Discussion Guide

In the following group discussion guide, I recommend some questions or activities for your group. You may not have time for all the questions, depending on your group size. Feel free to adjust these ideas in a way that best serves the needs of your group members.

Introductory Meeting

I recommend you have an introductory meeting before everyone begins week 1.

- Introduce yourselves to one another.

- Make sure everyone has a copy of this workbook. (Throughout the workbook, I recommend reading portions of my book *Understanding Spiritual Abuse: What It Is and How to Respond*, so it would be helpful if the group members have a copy of the book in addition to the workbook.)
- Set group expectations.
  - Set expectations for in-person groups.
  - Set additional recommendations if the group meets online (listed in the above section).
  - Read each expectation and have each member place a checkmark by each expectation that they agree to abide by the guidelines for the safety of members.
- Share your goals and hopes for participating in this group.
- Share concerns about participating in this group or completing the workbook.
- Look at the feelings chart in the back of this workbook. Go around the group, asking everyone to identify the emotions they are experiencing. Inform group members that we will use this chart at the beginning of each group session to allow members time to "check in" with how they are feeling. (We will explore the concept of emotions in week two.)
- Allow approximately ten to fifteen minutes for members to write a letter to themselves that they will read silently at the beginning of the last group session. (What do you hope to get out of this group? What do you want to say to yourself about completing this twelve-week journey? What might it look like to take steps toward healing?)
- Encourage group members to complete "What Is Spiritual Abuse?" (week 1) before meeting next week. Remind group members that if a portion of the assignments are too challenging to complete, they can skip those sections and save them for a later time.

Week 1: What Is Spiritual Abuse?

- Check in using the emotion chart.
- Share the words, phrases, or images that come to mind when you think of spiritual abuse.
- Read the definition of spiritual abuse. If you are comfortable doing so, and without sharing your entire story at this time, identify what type of setting your spiritual abuse occurred (i.e., church, discipleship setting, mission organization, family relationship).
- Discuss the concept of safe people. Describe characteristics you are looking for in a safe person. Are there any other traits you would add to the list?
- How has your experience of spiritual abuse impacted your ability to trust others?
- Share your favorite pleasurable activities. If you have any additional ideas, share them with the group. Continue to share throughout this group as you discover new grounding, coping, or pleasurable activities.
- Scripture: Read 1 Corinthians 13:1–13.
- Close the session with the group leader guiding the group through the 54321 exercise.
- Encourage group members to complete "Emotions Matter" (week 2) before the next session.

Week 2: Emotions Matter

- Check in using the emotion chart.
- Read Psalm 42 and discuss what emotion is expressed in this psalm.
- Discuss the messages you received about emotions when you were a child.
- Discuss the messages you received about emotions in the spiritually abusive experience.

- In the spiritually abusive experience, were emotions
  - overemphasized?
  - minimized?
  - used to manipulate?
- Describe one way this impacts your experience of emotions in your current experience.
- Discuss any pleasurable activities the group members have tried and any they recommend adding to the list.
- Encourage group members to complete "Safety and Identifying Triggers" (week 3) before the next group session.

Week 3: Safety and Identifying Triggers

- Check in using the emotion chart.
- Discuss the meaning of triggers.
- Allow time for group members to identify current spiritual symbols or activities that are triggers of the spiritually abusive situation.
- Describe boundaries. What are some benefits of having healthy boundaries?
- Discuss how your boundaries were violated in the spiritually abusive situation.
- Scripture: Allow each group member time to share the description of God that was the most comforting from the passages in day 6. Read the passages.
- Encourage group members to complete "Caught in a Web: Part 1" (week 4) before the next group session.

Week 4: Caught in a Web (Part 1)

- Check in using the emotion chart.
- In group this week, we will focus on four of the ways that a spiritual abuser entraps individuals in a web. Remember that not everyone

may experience each topic covered. Group members can participate as applicable.

1. A "good" beginning. Briefly describe what was "good" (if anything) about the beginning.
2. Self-appointed "divine" authority. Discuss how your spiritual abuser made "divine" claims.
3. The hypocrisy of not practicing what they teach. What expectations were placed on you that the spiritual abuser was unwilling to perform?
4. Legalist loads. What image comes to mind when you think of carrying these loads?

- How has the spiritually abusive experience impacted your image of God?
- Review the unhelpful thinking patterns and briefly discuss them.
- Read Philippians 2:3–11. Contrast the Christlike attitudes with that of the spiritual abuser.
- Practice the 478 breathing together before closing.
- Encourage group members to complete "Caught in a Web: Part 2" (week 5) before the group next week.

Week 5: Caught in a Web (Part 2)

- Check in using the emotion chart.
- We are continuing the discussion about ways the spiritual abuser weaves a web of control. Discuss the following four ways as applicable to group members.
    1. Deceptive use of God's name and Scripture. What Scripture or theological teachings were misused to control?
    2. Seeking self-promotion and praise. Discuss what was problematic about the attitudes and actions of the scribes and Pharisees in Matthew 23.

3. Focus on outward appearance. In Matthew 23:23–24, what "more important matters of the law" were neglected? What important matters were neglected in your spiritually abusive experience?
4. Instilling fear. Describe one fear that particularly stands out in your mind.

- Discuss the concept of anger using the anger iceberg analogy. What were you taught about anger in the spiritually abusive setting?
- Read Philippians 2:3–11. Describe how the spiritual abuser is nothing like Christ.
- Review the unhelpful thinking patterns and briefly discuss them.
- Conclude today by reading Psalm 23.
- Encourage group members to complete "Coercive and Manipulative Control: Part 1" (week 6) before the group next week.

Week 6: Coercive and Manipulative Control (Part 1)

- Check in using the emotion chart.
- This week, we will review three ways the spiritual abuser controls the victim.
    1. Control by limiting personal agency:
        a. Share one example of how your personal agency was controlled.
        b. Discuss how the control of decisions impacts your ability to make decisions today.
    2. Control by excessive accountability enforced by monitoring behavior:
        a. Describe healthy accountability.
        b. How is this different from the excessive accountability you experienced in the spiritually abusive setting?

3. Control by performance-based acceptance:
   a. In what areas were you expected to participate or "perform"?
   b. What was the consequence when you did not participate?

- ➢ Discuss members' experiences identifying values.
- ➢ Scripture: Invite members to share what they learned about wisdom and allow time for members to pray for wisdom.
- ➢ Encourage members to complete "Coercive and Manipulative Control: Part 2" (week 7) before group next week.

Week 7: Coercive and Manipulative Control (Part 2)

- ➢ Check in using the emotion chart.
- ➢ This week, we will review the three remaining ways the spiritual abuser might control the victims.
  1. Control by required obedience to the abuser: What happened if the spiritual abuser's power or control was threatened?
  2. Control by censuring. What questions did you want to ask but felt unsafe to do so?
  3. Control by isolation. If you were isolated, name one or two ways this impacts your relationships today.
- ➢ Since the time of your spiritually abusive experience, do you struggle with making decisions? If so, what is one decision you currently struggle to make (if you are comfortable sharing)?
- ➢ Scripture: How does the description of wisdom introduced in the passages this week differ from the attitude of the spiritual abuser?
- ➢ At this point, you are slightly past the halfway point of the workbook. Discuss with group members any challenges you are facing. Make adjustments that best suit the needs of your group members.
- ➢ Encourage group members to complete "Identifying Holistic Harm" (week 8) before the next session.

Week 8: Identifying Holistic Harm

- Check in using the emotion chart.
- This week focused on the areas of harm reflected in the Spiritual Abuse Assessment. Describe your experience of exploring the areas of harm in your life.
- Did any of the areas of harm surprise you? If so, please discuss.
- When reviewing the areas of harm (spiritual, emotional/psychological, relational, and physical), which area of harm stands out to you as the most difficult in your present circumstances?
- Describe what healing would look like in this area. How would things be different?
- Discuss the meaning of suffering and develop a definition based on the group's feedback.
- Review the steps of the prayer of lament.
- Using the steps of lament, lead the group through a prayer of lament. Be sensitive to those who may have difficulty doing this in a group setting and may need to excuse themselves. Members can complete this silently or aloud, allowing members time to participate in each step. If doing the prayer aloud, pause at each step to allow each person time to participate:
    1. Address God by calling out names of God.
    2. Voice specific emotions and complaints.
    3. Make a confession of trust.
    4. Make a request to God.
    5. Express a commitment to praise.

  Encourage members to complete "Your Spiritual Timeline" (week 9) before the group next week.

Week 9: Your Spiritual Timeline

- Check in using the emotion chart.
- Describe what it was like completing the spiritual timeline.

- ➢ Describe your first introduction to God.
- ➢ If you are comfortable doing so, share one challenging time in your spiritual journey.
- ➢ Share a positive experience from your spiritual journey.
- ➢ Share an experience from your spiritual history that deeply impacts your view of God. (This may be a positive experience or a challenging experience. If time allows, the group may decide to share one of each.)
- ➢ Have you struggled with "never good enough" thoughts? Name one way this currently impacts your life.
- ➢ Scripture: Read Isaiah 40:27–31. Allow members time to share what areas they need "strength" in. Pray for one another.
- ➢ Encourage group members to complete "Understanding Spiritual Health" (week 10) before next week.

Week 10: Understanding Spiritual Health

- ➢ Check in using the emotion chart.
- ➢ Invite group members to share how they define "spiritual health."
- ➢ How are emotional and spiritual health related?
- ➢ Read the quote by Scazzero. Has there been a time when God spoke to you through your emotions and physical responses?
- ➢ What practices are most helpful in your spiritual health?
- ➢ Review SMART goals. Invite group members to share their goals.
- ➢ Review the circles of control and invite members to share how they can apply this tool.
- ➢ Scripture: 1 Peter 5:1–5. Allow members time to share their cares and pray for one another.
- ➢ Encourage group members to complete "When Forgiveness Is Weaponized" (week 11) before next week.

Week 11: When Forgiveness Is Weaponized

- ➢ Check in using the emotion chart.
- ➢ Acknowledge the difficulty of exploring forgiveness. Invite members to share their concerns about discussing the topic. Discuss the following:
  - ❍ What do you believe forgiveness is "not"?
  - ❍ What is forgiveness?
  - ❍ What are the spiritual, emotional/psychological, relational, and physical consequences of the lack of forgiveness and holding resentment?
  - ❍ What are my reasons for forgiving?
  - ❍ Allow members time to explore forgiveness as it relates to their experience of spiritual abuse.
- ➢ Scripture: Read the passages from day 6 about the forgiveness of God. Allow members to discuss God's forgiveness.
- ➢ Encourage group members to complete "Characteristics of a Safe Community" (week 12) before next week.

Week 12: Characteristics of a Safe Community

- ➢ Check in using the emotion chart.
- ➢ Invite members to share their favorite coping skills.
- ➢ Review and discuss the eleven markers of a safe, healthy community.
- ➢ Allow members to share their takeaways from their experiences over the past twelve weeks.
- ➢ Provide time for the group members to silently read the letters they wrote to themselves during the introductory meeting. Allow time for discussion.
- ➢ Scripture: Read and discuss the passages in day 6. Allow members time to share passages that were meaningful in their healing journey up to this point.

Locate a Counselor

The following websites can be used to locate a counselor in your area:

- ➢ Psychology Today:
  - ❍ https://www.psychologytoday.com/us/therapists
- ➢ American Association for Marriage and Family Therapy:
  - ❍ https://www.aamft.org/directories/find_a_therapist.aspx
- ➢ Christian Association for Psychological Studies:
  - ❍ https://caps.net/online-directory/

The following website can be used to locate a therapist trained in Eye Movement Desensitization and Reprocessing (EMDR):

- ➢ EMDR International Association:
  - • https://www.emdria.org/find-an-emdr-therapist/